CENTRAL FISHERIES BOARD
IRISH ANGLING GUIDES

SeaAngling

NORMAN DUNLOP AND PETER GREEN

AREA INTRODUCTIONS BY DICK WARNER

G000245443

GILL AND MACMILLAN

Published in Ireland by
Gill and Macmillan Ltd
Goldenbridge
Dublin 8
with associated companies in Auckland, Budapest, Gaborone, Harare,
Hong Kong, Kampala, Kuala Lumpur, Lagos, London, Madras, Manzini,
Melbourne, Mexico City, Nairobi, New York, Singapore, Sydney,
Tokyo, Windhoek
© Central Fisheries Board 1992
0 7171 1825 8
Editorial Consultant Roberta Reeners
Design and Artwork by Design Image, Dublin
Print origination by Seton Music Graphics Ltd, Bantry, Co. Cork
Printed by The Guernsey Press Co. Ltd, Guernsey, C.I.
The maps are based on the Ordnance Survey by permission of the Government
(Permit No. 5552)
A catalogue record is available for this book from the British Library.

CONTENTS

SEA ANGLING

Central Fisheries Board
Irish Angling Guides

A totally comprehensive series of handbooks on every aspect of angling in Ireland. Compiled by and published in association with the Irish Fisheries Boards, each Guide provides all the most recent and accurate information required by the angler to make the most of Ireland's superb angling opportunities.

The series comprises three books:
Sea Angling
Coarse Angling
Game Angling

THE FISHERIES BOARDS

The Central and seven Regional Fisheries Boards were established to protect, develop and promote all forms of sport fishing in Ireland. They are non-profit-making bodies and all income, including the royalties from this book, is devoted to fishery improvement and conservation. The Central Board employs specialist Coarse, Game and Sea angling staff whose main function is the collection and dissemination of angling information such as is included here.

The Board wishes to thank its colleagues all over the country, the thousands of anglers, the boat operators, club secretaries, fishery owners and all those interested and involved in the sport without whose co-operation these guides could not be produced.

This guide was compiled by the Central Fisheries Board's two Sea Angling Advisers, Norman Dunlop and Peter Green.

INFORMATION

The nature of angling is such that the information provided must be viewed as being as accurate as possible at the time of going to print.

The Fisheries Boards provide maps, brochures and some local guides and Bord Failte, the Irish Tourist Board, provides a set of three brochures titled 'Only The Best' Coarse, Game and Sea Angling.

The Irish Tourist Board also inspects accommodation, registering and approving only the premises meeting its high standards. The Fisheries Boards recommend that anglers stay only at such approved accommodation. Guides and lists are available from any tourist office.

Ireland is Europe's outstanding sea angling destination. It offers wonderful fishing, a well-organised angling infrastructure, first-class accommodation to suit all tastes, and a warm-hearted, friendly people who are always happy to help you enjoy your sport.

Ireland has already hosted most of Europe's top sea angling events. Shore and boat angling competitions and festivals are held all around the coast, particularly during the weekends of summer and autumn. Since no part of the country is more than 110 km (70 miles) from the sea, an angling trip is never too difficult. Whether you are a competition angler, a serious specimen hunter or just fishing while on holiday, you are sure to enjoy yourself.

Our position in the extreme west of Europe is most conducive to good fishing. The warm waters of the North Atlantic Drift (an extension of the Gulf Stream) lap the south and west coasts and this is responsible for our mild climate – not too cold in winter and not too hot in summer. As a result, we get warm-water species such a Blue Shark and Bass mixing with the Cod and Coalfish and Porbeagle which prefer cooler waters. The result is a very varied and exciting fish population.

■ COASTLINE

The coastline too is extremely varied – 6000 km (3700 miles) of a magical mixture of deep bays, estuaries, huge rocky cliffs, quiet sheltered inlets, long flat storm beaches, steep-to-shingle shores and rocky ledges designed by nature years ago, especially for the comfort of today's shore anglers. Generally speaking, the sea off the east coast is shallower than the south coast, while the depths of the western seaboard drop dramatically at places such as Valentia and Belmullet, where the 100 metre line and the continental slope are closest to the landmass.

■ TIDES

On all parts of the Irish coast, there are two High Tides and two Low Tides in each period of 24 hours, 50 minutes. 'Double tides' are encountered only in a small stretch south of Dublin on the east coast. High Water at Dublin occurs about half an hour before High Water at Dover. In general, High Water on the south and west coasts occurs about six hours before High Water at Dublin. High Water at Wicklow is three-quarters of an hour and at Courtown, 3½ hours earlier than Dublin. Spring tides at Dublin are mid-day tides (HW). They are evening tides (approx. 6 pm) on the south and west. The height at spring tide varies from approximately 0.9 m (3ft) at Arklow to 4.9 m (16 ft) at Foynes and Galway. Tide times are published in the national daily papers.

■ THE SPORT

It is almost certain that the sport of sea angling started on the south coast at Ballycotton with the arrival of a London-based Sea Angling Club called the 'Dreadnoughts' in the early 1900s. They fished the area every summer through the 1920s and '30s until the war intervened. Their records, which still exist, reveal tremendous fishing for Shark, Skate, Ling, Pollack etc.

The sport got a great boost in the early 1950s when the Irish Federation of Sea Anglers was established. This body is still the strongest voice of the sport in Ireland and today has 200 affiliated clubs. Deep sea angling centres such as Kinsale and Westport led the field in catering for tourists, especially those interested in deep sea angling. Through the 1960s places like the Dingle Peninsula and Co. Clare became world famous for quality shore angling – Dingle for its Bass fishing on the magnificent storm beaches and Clare for its rock fishing for a variety of species including shore-caught Porbeagle Shark. Today, Ireland boasts some fifty centres catering for the whole spectrum of sea angling, from shore fishing through inshore (small boat) angling to deep sea fishing from specially-equipped charter vessels.

■ SHORE ANGLING

This is by far the most popular form of the sport. It is enjoyed all around the coast, but is most popular south of a line from Galway to Dublin. It can be divided into three forms – Beach, Rock and Pier fishing, each with a particular appeal. Beach anglers generally seek Bass, Ray, Flounder and Codling, while rock anglers seek Pollack, Wrasse, Conger, Mackerel and Ray. Pier fishermen mostly take Mullet, Dogfish, Ray, Conger and Flounder. On occasion, it may be necessary for shore anglers to cross private property to reach angling stations. This should only be done after permission has been secured.

■ INSHORE ANGLING

This is carried out from small 13–20 ft (4–6 m) boats, usually fitted with outboard engines. It is normally confined to sheltered bays and inlets. Some anglers tow their own boats and launch them from any of the hundreds of piers and slipways as they motor around the country. In some areas, these boats can be hired locally. This form of the sport is most common on the east coast, but is growing in popularity on the south and west coasts where there are numerous safe bays and estuaries. All species of fish are sought, but generally Cod,

Ray, Plaice, Monkfish, Pollack and Tope are the most important.

■ DEEP SEA ANGLING

Of the three forms of sea angling available, this is the one on which Ireland's reputation is based. Deep sea angling necessitates the use of specially-equipped seagoing launches of 26–40 ft (8 – 12 m). These boats can be chartered for approximately £70 to £100 per day, or an angler can book a place on board for approximately £10 to £18 per day. The boats usually take seven to eight anglers, depending on the type of fishing sought, i.e. ground (bottom) fishing or shark fishing. The species caught in deep water will, of course, be similar to those in the shore and inshore categories, but tend to be larger. However, to these we add Blue and Porbeagle Shark, Big Skate, Ray and Ling. Tackle can be hired in most centres for about £5 per day. The boats usually go out at about 9 or 10 am and return at 6 or 7 pm. In recent times, the charter boat owners and skippers have formed an organisation called ISAAC (Irish Sea Angling Accommodation and Charters). This group's aim is to maintain standards of service at the highest level, and to promote the Irish Sea Angling industry abroad. All boats listed in this guide are Bord Failte (Irish Tourist Board) approved. Each vessel flies a green flag emblazoned with a shamrock to indicate that the boat has complied with the standards and regulations as laid down by the Tourist Board. This list may change from time to time. If in doubt check with Bord Failte, Baggot Street, Dublin 2. We would advise visiting anglers to use the angling facilities of those boats which display this flag.

■ COMPETITIONS AND ANGLING FESTIVALS

The Irish Federation of Sea Anglers (IFSA) and its constituent Provincial Councils organise, through its member clubs, a great number of boat and shore competitions all around the coast. They range from one day to week-long events. Some run for a few days, others are held over a weekend. Enjoyable fringe events of a social nature are also organised, making them great festivals of sea angling. These events complement the good fishing which is also there for sampling on days that are free from competition.

Details of all IFSA competitions are available in 'Gaff', the official publication of the IFSA, from the Hon. Secretary, IFSA, 67 Windsor Drive, Monkstown, Co. Dublin, or from any affiliated club.

The Irish Match Angling & Surf Casting Association (IMASA) also organise shore angling matches for the more specialised shore anglers. Valuable cash prizes are usually awarded at these events. Details from Hon. Secretary, IMASA, 80 Moreen Avenue, Sandyford, Dublin 16, (01) 952157.

Conservation is now a very important feature in all of the competitions fished in Ireland. Most have their own sets of conservation rules which generally insist on the fish being returned alive to the water.

◼ CONSERVATION AND TAGGING

The majority of Irish charter skippers are participating in a Marine Sportfish Tagging Programme run by the Central Fisheries Board. Of major importance are Shark, Tope, Monkfish and all the Rays. The programme is designed to gather information on the movements and habits of these species which are very important to the Irish angling industry. The skippers measure and tag each fish with its own individual number to trace its movements. Tags are returned from all over the North Atlantic between America, North Africa and the Mediterranean. Many fish have been caught and released numerous times. All anglers are requested to assist skippers, where possible, in returning all cartilaginous fish alive to the water.

Results from the tagging programme have shown that certain sedentary species, such as Skate and Ray, are liable to overfishing by both commercial operations and by anglers. Of particular interest is the Common Skate *(Raja batis)*. In the interests of its conservation, the Irish Specimen Fish Committee removed the Common Skate from its list of eligible species in 1977. The response to the committee's appeal to anglers to conserve this species was very gratifying and now virtually all angling centres around the country return these huge fish unharmed to the water. As a result, the species is making a remarkable comeback in some areas.

Bass *(Dicentrarchus labrax)* is also under threat and the government has recently introduced legislation whereby a daily Bass limit of two fish per angler was brought into operation and the commercial capture and sale of Bass was prohibited. There is also a minimum size limit of 40 cm (16 in) total length. A closed season operated from 15 May to 15 June 1991 and it is hoped that this closed season (spawning time) will continue in future years. Anglers are requested to respect this law as adherence should improve future sport.

■ BASS* *(Dicentrarchus labrax)*

This blue-backed, silvery, hard-scaled cousin of the American Striped Bass is one of Ireland's most sought-after sport fish. It is found in various locations and is equally at home in the turmoil of an Atlantic surf beach or in the quietness of an estuarine backwater or creek.

Most common below a line drawn from Galway to Dublin, but localised populations exist beyond this area. Grows to around 20 lbs (9 kg). Season fished is generally from May to October.

Irish Specimen Weight: 10 lbs (4.5 kg)

*For information on conservation bye-law, see previous page.

■ COALFISH *(Pollachius virens)*

Common on all coasts. Can be identified from its near relative, the Pollack, by the forked tail fin and straight lateral line. Coloration is dark green or blackish green above and paler on the sides. Small Coalfish, locally named 'Glassaun', 'Blockin' etc. can be a nuisance at times but larger fish, 10 lbs+ (4.5 kg+) offer good sport, particularly on light tackle. Normally found in the vicinity of reefs or sunken wrecks, especially where there is a fair run of tides. Grows to about 40 lbs (18 kg).

Irish Specimen Weight: 15 lbs (6.8 kg)

■ COD *(Gadus morhua)*

Common on most coasts of Ireland, this popular angling and culinary fish is unlikely to be mistaken for any other species, even though the colour of adults varies from greenish grey to red-brown, depending on the area inhabited. The lower jaw sports a well-developed barbel. Can be expected over a wide range of seabed, from reefs and wrecks to areas of shingle and sand. Has a good tolerance for brackish water and is known to exist in many of the larger estuaries. Cod are available throughout much of the year, but generally the 'peak' fishing times are May and June (boat angling) and December and January (shore angling). Grows to over 50 lbs (22.7 kg).

Irish Specimen Weight: 25 lbs (11 kg)

■ CONGER *(Conger conger)*

Common on most coasts, this large-mouthed, muscular eel is a popular quarry with many anglers. However, Congers should always be treated with respect, particularly the bigger specimens, as they can be dangerous at close quarters, especially when provoked. In shallow water, the Conger is dark brown to black on the back, while fish from deeper water are generally grey or fawn in colour. Frequents areas of rocky ground, harbour walls and sunken wrecks. Grows to over 100 lbs (45 kg).

Irish Specimen Weight: 40 lbs (18 kg)

■ DOGFISH *(Families: Scyliorhinidae and Squalidae)*

There are three species of dogfish in Irish waters, i.e. Greater Spotted Dogfish *(Scyliorhinus stellaris)*, Lesser Spotted Dogfish *(Scyliorhinus caniculus)* and Spurdog *(Squalus acanthias)*. All are small members of the shark family and all are common on most coasts. Lesser Spotted Dogfish grow to about 4 lbs (1.8 kg) and are widely distributed, being particularly prolific in the larger bays. Greater Spotted Dogfish grow to over 20 lbs (9 kg) and are also found in

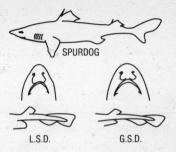

large bays, but they generally prefer deeper water. Spurdog which also grow to around 20 lbs (9 kg) have become less common in recent years, but are still found, in large numbers at times, on the western seaboard, particularly during the summer months.

■ FLOUNDER *(Platichthys flesus)*

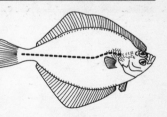

Most common of all Irish flatfishes. Can be found on coasts where there are areas of sand or mud close to the shoreline. Often found in numbers high up estuaries and in freshwater outflows.

Popular with shore anglers, particularly in competitions where their free feeding habits make them easy to catch. Conspicuous, rough, hard scales behind head and along top to lateral line. Dark brown or olive on upper side, sometimes showing pale orange spots. Grows to about 5 lbs (2.2 kg).

Irish Specimen Weight: 3 lbs (1.3 kg)

■ GURNARD *(Family: Triglidea)*

There are three species of Gurnard which anglers can expect from Irish waters. They are Grey Gurnard *(Eutrigla gurnardus)* which grows to about 3.5 lbs (1.6 kg); Red Gurnard *(Aspitrigla cuculus)* which grows to about 4 lbs (1.8 kg); and Tub Gurnard *(Trigla lucerna)*

which grows to over 12 lbs (5 kg). Gurnards are bottom-living fishes, normally found on sandy or muddy bottoms in depths of 50-150 feet, and are particularly common on the western seaboard.

■ LING *(Molva molva)*

Long, eel-like member of the Cod family which has a large barbel under the chin and a mouth of needle-sharp teeth. Olive or red-brown in colour, sometimes mottled. A very popular sport fish with wreck and reef anglers. Almost exclusively a boat-caught species. Grows to about 50 lbs (23 kg).

Irish Specimen Weight: 25 lbs (11 kg)

■ MACKEREL *(Scomber scombrus)*

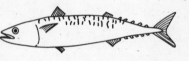

Very common in summer when they can be taken by anglers, in numbers at times, from both boat and shore. Easily identified by characteristic dark wavy stripes on green upper body and silver undersides. Two small keels on each side of tail fin. Grows to about 6 lbs (2.7 kg).

Irish Specimen Weight: 2.5 lbs (1 kg)

■ MONKFISH *(Squatina squatina)*

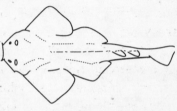

Large, ugly, squat, carti-laginous fish which resembles a cross between a Shark and a Skate. Dark brown in colour. Frequents shallow water, particularly on the west coast of Ireland, i.e. Tralee Bay, Clew Bay and Blacksod Bay. Grows to around 100 lbs (45 kg).

Irish Specimen Weight: 50 lbs (23 kg)

■ MULLET, GREY-THICK LIPPED
(Crenimugil labrosus)

Often seen cruising in shoals close to the surface in tidal stretches of rivers, estuaries and harbours during the summer months. Broad-backed 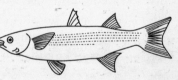 with shortish head and small, triangular mouth. Greyish-silver in colour with dark, horizontal streaks. Grows to over 10 lbs (4.5 kg).

Irish Specimen Weight: 5 lbs (2.2 kg)

■ PLAICE *(Pleuronectes platessa)*

Very popular angling and culinary fish. Common on the east and south coasts, less common in the west. Prefers ground where sand or shingle banks are located. Can be caught from both boat and 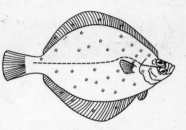 shore. The scales are smooth, with a row of bony knobs behind the eyes. Brownish in colour, with well-defined red or deep orange spots. Grows to 10 lbs (4.5 kg).

Irish Specimen Weight: 4 lbs (1.8 kg)

■ POLLACK *(Pollachius pollachius)*

Very popular sport fish. Can be taken from both boat and shore on most coasts, particularly over areas  of rough ground. Less common in the Irish Sea. Easily identified from its near relation, the Coalfish, by the protruding lower jaw and by the shape of the lateral line which is bent over the pectoral fin. Tail not forked. Usually brown or bronze on back. Grows to over 20 lbs (9 kg).

Irish Specimen Weight: 12 lbs (5.4 kg)

■ RAY FAMILY *(Raja)*

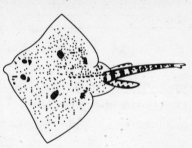

There are eight species of ray which are common to Irish waters. They are Thornback *(Raja clavata)*: Irish Specimen Weight: 20 lbs (9 kg); Blonde Ray *(Raja brachyura)*: Irish Specimen Weight: 25 lbs (11 kg); Cuckoo Ray *(Raja naevus)*: Irish Specimen Weight: 4.5 lbs (2 kg); Electric Ray *(Torpedo nobiliana)*: Irish Specimen Weight: 20 lbs (9 kg); Homelyn Ray *(Raja montagui)*: Irish Specimen Weight: 5 lbs (2 kg); Undulate Ray *(Raja undulata)*: Irish Specimen Weight: 14 lbs (6 kg); Painted Ray *(Raja microcellata)*: Irish Specimen Weight: 10 lbs (4.5 kg); Sting Ray *(Dasyatis pastinaca)*: Irish Specimen Weight: 30 lbs (13.6 kg).

The majority of Irish Rays are found in fairly shallow water and are popular sport fish for both boat and shore anglers. Generally, Ray are summer species, being available from May to October.

■ SKATE, COMMON *(Raja batis)*

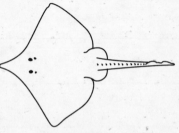

The largest of three known species of Skate found in Irish waters. The other smaller skates are the White *(Raja alta)* and the Long Nosed *(Raja oxyrinchus)*. At one time, Common Skate were available all round the coast, but concentrated fishing by anglers was blamed for a marked decline in the late 1960s. As a result, the Irish Specimen Fish Committee removed the Common Skate from its list of acceptable species in an effort to conserve the remaining stocks. Today, virtually all charter skippers return Skate alive to the water and in the last few years, the species appears to be re-establishing itself in several venues.

Irish specimen weight suspended

■ SMOOTH HOUND *(Mustelus asterias)*

During the mid 1980s, this fish became something of a cult species with anglers fishing on the North Wexford coast. Sporadic reports have been received from other centres, but to date, the Smooth Hound has only been positively identified from the east coast. This inshore shark provides excellent sport on light tackle, particularly in springtime, and is somewhat like a smaller version of a Tope. The teeth of the Smooth Hound are barred (similar to Ray) and this distinguishes them from their larger brethren. Grows to about 20 lbs (9 kg).

Irish Specimen Weight: 7 lbs (3 kg)

■ TOPE *(Galeorhinus galeus)*

Small to medium sized shallow water shark, fairly common on all coasts of Ireland during the summer. Greyish in colour with short triangular pectorals and a deeply notched tail fin. Extremely popular sport fish, particularly with small inshore boat anglers. Often male fish of 30 lbs (13.6 kg) or so are encountered in 'packs' (Dingle, Westport, Blacksod and Lough Swilly), but the much larger females are usually in smaller groups or may even be 'loners'. Grows to about 80 lbs (36 kg).

Irish Specimen Weight: 40 lbs (18 kg)

■ TURBOT *(Scophthalmus maximus)*

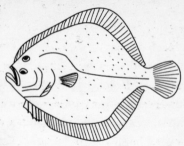

Large flatfish, the capture of which is regarded by many anglers as one of the major prizes of Irish sea angling. Highly regarded also for the table, as the flaky white, subtly flavoured flesh has few peers. Upper side is mottled brown with numerous bony lumps or tubercles. The body is diamond shaped. Grows to over 40 lbs (18 kg).

Irish Specimen Weight: 18 lbs (8 kg)

■ WHITING *(Merlangius merlangus)*

Common member of Cod family. Three dorsal, two anal fins. Upper jaw the longer; no barbel. Tail-fin not forked. Lateral line a narrow, brown seam. Pinkish-brown above, silvery on the sides. Grows to about 6 lbs (2.7 kg).

Irish Specimen Weight: 3 lbs (1.36 kg)

■ BALLAN WRASSE *(Labrus bergylta)*

In this and in most species of Wrasse, the body is fairly deep, but not excessively compressed and it is covered with hard scales. There is a single, long dorsal fin, with spines in the anterior portion; anal fin of moderate length, with spines anteriorly. Tail broad and somewhat rounded; pectorals broad and rounded. No spines on gill-cover; lips thick and fleshy; jaws with powerful conical teeth. Common over rocky ground, particularly in the west.

Irish Specimen Weight: 4.75 lbs (2.1 kg)

■ BLUE SHARK *(Prionace glauca)*

Very popular sport fish, particularly on south and west coasts. Slender shark with small gill-slits, raked-back tail and very long slender pectorals. Teeth triangular, with a finely serrated cutting edge. Vivid blue above when freshly caught. Grows to several hundred pounds in weight.

Irish Specimen Weight: 100 lbs (45 kg)

■ PORBEAGLE *(Lamna nasus)*

Body stout, gill-slits and eye rather large. Tail-fin set vertically, with the upper lobe somewhat the larger. A keel on each side of the tail column and a smaller secondary keel on the tail below it. Second dorsal fin is small, placed over the anal fin. Teeth long, slender with (in the adult) small secondary cusps at their base. Brownish or greyish. Grows to over 400 lbs (180 kg). Fairly common on western seaboard.

Irish Specimen Weight: 140 lbs (68 kg)

BAITS

Depending on the quarry, an angler will require some of the following.

◼ LUGWORM

Abundant in estuaries and on most sheltered beaches throughout Ireland. The presence of lugworm can be ascertained by the spaghetti-like spiral of sand which they leave on the foreshore at low tide.

Trench digging for an hour or so with a garden fork will normally produce enough worms for a day's fishing. In Ireland, lugworm have traditionally been a shore angler's bait, usually associated with fishing for Flounder, Wrasse, Dabs etc., but they are also very effective in attracting Codling and Whiting while inshore boat fishing.

◼ RAGWORM

Although quite common on the eastern seaboard, Red and King Ragworm are absent from most of the west coast of Ireland and anglers wishing to use these baits must be prepared to carry a supply with them. These ragworm can be an excellent bait while shore or boat fishing for Flatfish, Whiting, Pouting, Codling and Dogfish.

Harbour Ragworm or 'Maddies' are very common in the muddy reaches of most estuaries. These small ragworm are a good standby bait for float fishing for Mullet or ledgering for Flatfish.

White Ragworm or 'Herringbone rag' are also common, frequenting many lugworm beds. They are particularly effective when used in conjunction with other baits such as lugworm or mackerel strip.

Large White Ragworm or 'Silvers' are rare and very localised in their distribution throughout the entire country.

They are, however, the singular most sought-after bait by shore match anglers who tend to jealously guard the location of 'silver' beds. Large white ragworm are often the only bait that will attract fish in bright conditions and many shore competitions have been won by the angler with a good supply of them. They are normally found in clean, coarse sand in the vicinity of the low spring tide line, particularly where masonary worms (which have little use as bait) are located.

■ CRAB

The Common Shore or Green Crab moults at least once a year, usually prior to mating. This generally takes place in May or June, although moulting crabs have been found as late as October in some places. Crabs can be collected along sheltered shores, particularly where there is an abundance of serrated wrack which provides good cover for them. Not all shore crabs are suitable as baits and only 'peelers' or 'softies' are usable.

A 'Peeler Crab' is one which is in the process of shedding its shell and is generally regarded as the prime crab bait. To tell a 'Peeler' from an ordinary hard-backed crab, one should twist the last segment off one of the legs. If the segment comes away and there is white flesh underneath, the crab is unsuitable and can be returned to its hiding place. If, however, the segment comes away easily, revealing the newly-formed, soft red flesh underneath, the carapace and undershell can be peeled off and you then have an excellent bait.

Crabs which have already shed their shell but have not yet hardened (a process which takes about a week) are known as 'Softies'. They are rubbery to the touch and cannot nip as the claws have not hardened enough to do any damage.

In most conditions, a soft crab will be almost as effective as a 'Peeler', although the 'scent' will not be as strong.

Crab can be used in almost any sea angling situation, from shore fishing, where they are effective for virtually all species, through inshore boat fishing for Ray, Dogfish and Flatfish, to deep sea fishing for Cod.

COCKLES

Cockles can be gathered in quantity on many parts of the coastline and are extremely useful for shore and inshore fishing especially when Plaice, Dabs and Flounder are the targets. They are also a very good bait for larger fish when used in a 'cocktail' with lugworm. Cod and Whiting find this combination very attractive.

CLAMS

The Common Gaper is oval-shaped and dark grey to black in colour and is found in muddy creeks and estuaries. It can be detected by searching for a keyhole-shaped depression in the mud. The hole is created by a long syphon with which the gaper filters small food particles out of the water.

Clams can be dug up with a fork and when the syphon is removed, it provides a very good boat angling bait for a number of species. Used in combination with lugworm or ragworm it is also a useful shore anglers' bait for Bass and Flatfish.

MUSSELS

Can be collected from most rocky shorelines but, because of the softness of their flesh, are used almost solely by boat anglers who do not need to cast a line to reach fish. If it is necessary to cast mussel, they should be tied to the hook with shirring elastic (elasticated thread). This can be very effective when fishing at short range from the shore, particularly on the east coast.

RAZORFISH

An excellent boat and shore bait, but they can only be obtained at low water of Spring tide strips.

Razors live in a burrow up to 3 feet (1 m) deep, usually in coarse sand, and are difficult to dig because the slightest movement on the sand above sends them spurting to the bottom of their hole. The most effective way of collecting razors is to use a long ½ inch diameter steel bar which has been flattened and shaped like an arrowhead at one end. When a razorfish burrow has been located, the steel rod should be rammed down the hole and twisted into the razor's shell. The rod is then withdrawn, hopefully with razor attached.

Razors can be used as bait for most summer species, but can also be very effective for winter Cod.

■ MACKEREL

The most important of all sea angling baits, Mackerel can be used for almost every species of fish from both boat and shore. It can be used in 'strip' form for Turbot, Megrim, Pollack, Coalfish or Gurnard. It is used in 'last' form (the tough tail section) for Ray, Bull Huss, Spurdog etc., and a half or whole Mackerel is used for Tope, Shark and Skate. Mackerel can be bought in most fish shops in season, or can usually be caught while spinning from harbour walls or rocky outcrops. While boat fishing, a string of brightly-coloured Mackerel feathers is employed to catch Mackerel in numbers. In recent years, there has been a marked decline in inshore stocks of Mackerel but generally an hour's searching can still provide ample supplies.

■ SANDEEL

An excellent bait for estuarine Sea Trout and Bass and for Pollack, Mackerel, Turbot, Dogfish and Rays from the boat.

Sandeel can be collected by the Cornish system known as 'Vingelling' in the wet sand with an old bill hook or long knife. The bill hook should be pulled in a sweep through the top six inches of sand and when a sandeel is located, it will wriggle out to the surface. Speed and dexterity are then called for to grab the fish and place it in a bucket.

Sandeel will stay alive in a bucket of cool, aerated sea water for several days.

■ ARTIFICIAL LURES

The types and designs of artificial lures are legion. However, the most useful in Irish waters are as follows.

SALTWATER SPINNING LURES: These are metal lures which wobble, shine and spin and are usually heavier than their freshwater counterparts. Good for Bass, Pollack and Coalfish in large size (21 cm). Smaller editions good for Mackerel and Sea Trout.

IMITATION SANDEELS: (ex. Redgills and Eddystone Eels) The best size is about 7 in. (18 cm) and they usually come in red, green, black or amber. They are good for Pollack, Coalfish etc. They should be of soft rubber and should wriggle well when moved slowly through the water.

PIRKS: Heavy, bright-coloured metal lures, usually with a large treble hook attached. Used jigging in deep water for Cod, Ling, Coalfish, Pollack etc.

FEATHERS: These come in a variety of sizes and designs and are used in strings of up to six at a time. Used jigging for Mackerel, Pollack or Coalfish. Can be baited with Mackerel or lugworm to catch a variety of species. The recently introduced 'Haikai' feathers with small, luminous fishlike heads, have proven very effective for a wide range of species.

■ SPECIMEN AND RECORD FISH

The Irish Specimen Fish Committee consists of representatives of the various angling federations, government departments and official organisations with an interest in Irish angling. Its objective is to verify records and publicise the capture on rod and line of Record and 'Specimen' fish in Irish waters. A list of specimen fish is published annually and is available from Hon. Secretary, Irish Specimen Fish Committee at the Central Fisheries Board, Glasnevin, Dublin 9.

Only fish which can be fully vouched for as to weight and species can be accepted. Specimen awards are presented annually, usually at functions in Dublin and Belfast.

Claim forms are available from the Hon. Secretary, or from local clubs and tackle shops. The following is a schedule of Record and Specimen Weights.

FRESHWATER SPECIES

SPECIES	WEIGHT LBS OZ		DATE OF CAPTURE	PLACE OF CAPTURE	CAPTOR
Salmon	57	0	1874	River Suir	M. Maher
Sea Trout	16	6	29.10.1983	Shimna River, Co. Down	Thomas McManus
Brown Trout (River)	20	0	22.2.1957	River Shannon, Corbally	Major Hugh Place
Brown Trout (Lake)	26	2	15.7.1894	Lough Ennel	Wm. Mears
Bream	11	12	1882	River Blackwater, (Monaghan)	A. Pike
Carp	26	2	28.5.1989	The Lough, Cork	Kieron V. Bend
Dace	1	2	8.8.1966	River Blackwater, Cappoquin	John T. Henry
Perch	5	8	1946	Lough Erne	S. Drum
Pike (River)	42	0	22.3.1964	River Barrow	M. Watkins
Pike (Lake)	38	2	25.2.1973	Lough Corrib	Brendan Hardiman
Roach	2	13½	11.8.1970	River Blackwater, Cappoquin	Lawrie Robinson
Rudd	3	4	27.5.1991	Annaghmore Lough	Steve Wilks
Rudd/Bream Hybrid	6	4	5.3.1990	Monalty Lake	Peter Walsh
Roach/Bream Hybrid	2.06 kg		2.7.1989	Drumreask L.	Philip Arthur
Tench	7	13¼	25.5.1971	River Shannon, Lanesboro	Raymond Webb
River Eel	6	15	12.6.1979	L. Droumenisa, Bantry	J. Murnane

MARINE SPECIES

SPECIES	WEIGHT LBS OZ	DATE OF CAPTURE	PLACE OF CAPTURE	CAPTOR
Angler Fish	42.985 kg	3.11.1985	Belfast Lough	Sean Neill
Bass	17 1¼	27.4.1977	Whiting Bay, Ardmore	Malcolm Tucker
Black Sole	6.32	28.12.1986	Ballycotton	Eddie Cull
Brill	9 8	8.9.1984	Causeway Coast	Deborah Gregg
Coalfish	12.5 kg	21.9.1983	Kinsale	E. Masheijer
Cod	42 0	1921	Ballycotton	I. L. Stewart
Conger	72 0	June 1914	Valentia	J. Green
Dab	2.02	28.1.1989	Dunmore East	Paul Beglin
Spur Dogfish	18 12	10.9.1977	Bantry	John Murnane
Greater Spotted Dogfish	23 12	29.5.1983	Valentia	Tony Outmayjer

SPECIES	WEIGHT LBS OZ	DATE OF CAPTURE	PLACE OF CAPTURE	CAPTOR
Lesser Spotted Dogfish	4 4	26.7.1982	Valentia	Cor Heinis
Flounder	4.60	9.11.1991	Ballyteigue	Patrick Cassidy
Garfish	3·10¼	16.9.1967	Kinsale	Even Bazard
Tub Gurnard	12 3½	8.8.1973	Bullsmouth, Achill	Robert Seaman
Grey Gurnard	3 1	21.9.1967	Rosslare Bay	Brendan Walsh
Red Gurnard	3 9½	17.7.1968	Belmullet	James Prescott
Haddock	10 13½	15.7.1964	Kinsale	F.A.E. Bull
Hake	25 5½	28.4.1962	Belfast Lough	H.W. Steele
Halibut	156	23.7.1972	Belmullet	Frank Brogan
Herring .	.425 kg	11.7.1986	Rathlin Island	Wm. McMath
John Dory	7 8	12.8.1984	Killala Bay	Cleona Walkin
Ling	46 8	26.7.1965	Kinsale	A.J.C. Bull
Mackerel	4 2	18.9.1979	Ballycotton	Ulrich Plassmann
Megrim	1.85 kg	26.7.1987	Killala	Paul Hennigan
Monkfish	73 0	1.6.1980	Fenit	James Boyd
Grey Mullet	7 10	8.6.1972	Killybegs Pier	Kevin Boyle
Plaice	8.23	23.1.1982	Ballycotton Pier	Edmund Cull
Pollack	19 3	1904	Ballycotton	J.N. Hearne
Pouting	4 13½	2.4.1983	Kilmore Quay	John Devereaux
Thornback Ray	37 0	28.5.1961	Ling Rocks, Kinsale	M.J. Fitzgerald
Blonde Ray	36 8	9.9.1964	Cork Harbour	D. Minchin
Sting Ray	51 0	8.8.1970	Fenit	John White
Cuckoo Ray	5 11	3.8.1975	Causeway Coast	V. Morrison
Undulate Ray	18	11.6.1977	Fenit	Ann-Mari Liedecke
Homelyn Ray	8.28	28.9.1983	Cork Harbour	Edmund Cull
Painted Ray	14.37	18.6.1980	Garryvoe	Edmund Cull
Electric Ray	69	5.9.1977	Courtmacsherry	J. Rynsburger
Ray's Bream	6 4¼	26.8.1979	Valentia	Martin Sarney
Red Sea Bream	9 6	24.8.1963	Valentia	P. Maguire
Twaite Shad	2.87	5.5.1985	St Mullins	Peter McCartin
Porbeagle Shark	365	1932	Keem Bay, Achill	Dr O'Donel Brown
Blue Shark	206	7.10.1959	Achill Head	J. McMonagle
Six Gilled Shark	154	28.8.1968	Kinsale	Andrew Bull
Common Skate	221	1913	Ballycotton	T. Tucker
White Skate	165	7.8.1966	Clew Bay	Jack Stack
Scad	1.97	6.9.1986	Clonakilty	Master R. McCarthy
Smooth Hound	13.75	27.6.1991	Five Mile Pt.	Peter Mooney
Stone Basse	10 13	2.8.1989	Kinsale	Stefano D'Amico
Three Bearded Rockling	3 1	11.5.90	Arklow	Maurice Laurent
Tope	66 8	15.7.1979	Carlingford Lough	Cyril Young
Torsk	4.7 kg	20.5.1989	Burtonport	Colin Hutton

Turbot	34	9.6.1982	Cork Harbour	Frank Fleming
Whiting	4 14½	19.3.1981	Kenmare Bay	Comdt. M.J. O'Connor
Ballan Wrasse	4.3 kg	20.8.1983	Clogher Head	Bertrand Kron
Cuckoo Wrasse	1.94	24.8.1991	Carne	Cecil Barron

■ SCHEDULE OF SPECIMEN WEIGHTS (REVISED)

FRESHWATER FISH	IRISH RECORD		SPECIMEN WEIGHT	
	LBS	OZ	LBS	KG
Salmon *(Salmo salar)*	57	0	20	9.072
Sea Trout *(Salmo trutta)*	16	6	6	2.721
Brown Trout *(Salmo trutta) (River)*	20	0	5	2.268
Brown Trout *(Salmo trutta) (Lake)*	26	2	10	4.536
Slob Trout *(Salmo trutta)*	–	–	10	4.536
Bream *(Abramis brama)*	11	12	7½	3.402
Carp *(Cyprinus carpio)*	26	2	10	4.536
Dace *(Leuciscus leuciscus)*	1	2	1	.454
Perch *(Perca fluviatilis)*	5	8	3	1.361
Pike *(Esox lucius) (Lake)*	38	2	30	13.608
Pike *(Esox lucius) (River)*	42	0	20	9.072
Roach *(Rutilus rutilus)*	2	13½	2	.907
Rudd *(Scardinius erythrophthalmus)*	3	1	2¼	1.021
Rudd/Bream hybrid	6	4	3	1.361
Roach/Bream hybrid	2.065 kg		3	1.361
Tench *(Tinca tinca)*	7	13¼	6	2.721
Eel *(Anguilla anguilla)*	6	15	3	1.361

SEA FISH	IRISH RECORD		SPECIMEN WEIGHT	
	LBS	OZ	LBS	KG
Angler fish *(Lophius piscatorius)*	42.985 kg		40	18.144
Bass *(Dicentrarchus labrax)*	17	1¼	10	4.536
Black Sole *(Solea solea)*	6.32		2	.907
Brill *(Scophthalmus rhombus)*	9	8	5	2.268
Coalfish *(Pollachius virens)*	12.5 kg		15	6.804
Cod *(Gadus morhua)*	42	0	25	11.340
Conger *(Conger conger)*	72	0	40	18.144
Dab *(Limanda limanda)*	2.02		1½	.680
Dogfish				
– Spur *(Squalus acanthias)*	18	12	12	5.443
– Lesser Spotted *(Scyliorhinus caniculus)*	4	4	3½	1.587
– Greater Spotted *(Scyliorhinus stellaris)*	23	12	16	7.257

SEA FISH	IRISH RECORD		SPECIMEN WEIGHT	
	LBS	OZ	LBS	KG
Flounder *(Platichthys flesus)*	4.60		3	1.361
Garfish *(Belone belone)*	3	10¼	2¼	1.021
(Belone svetovidovi)	1	0	14 oz	.355
Gurnard – Tub *(Trigla lucerna)*	12	3½	5	2.268
– Grey *(Eutrigla gurnardus)*	3	1	1½	.680
– Red *(Aspitigla cuculus)*	3	9½	2	.907
Haddock *(Melanogrammus aeglifinus)*	10	13½	7	3.175
Hake *(Merluccius merluccius)*	25	5 ½	10	4.536
Halibut *(Hippoglossus hippoglossus)*	156	0	50	22.680
Herring *(Culpea harengus)*	.425 kg		¾	.340
John Dory *(Zeus faber)*	7	8	4	1.814
Ling *(Molva molva)*	46	8	25	11.340
Mackerel *(Scomber scombrus)*	4	2	2½	1.134
Megrim *(Lepidorhombus whiffiagonis)*	1.85 kg		1¾	.794
Monkfish *(Squatina squatina)*	73	0	50	22.680
Mullet – Grey, thick lipped *(Crenimugil labrosus)*	7	10	5	2.268
– Red *(Mullus surmuletus)*	–	–	1	.454
Plaice *(Pleuronectes platessa)*	8.23		4	1.814
Pollack *(Pollachius pollachius)*	19	3	12	5.443
Pouting *(Trisopterus luscus)*	4	13½	3	1.361
Ray – Thornback *(Raja clavata)*	37	0	20	9.072
– Blonde *(Raja brachyura)*	36	8	25	11.340
– Cuckoo *(Raja naevus)*	5	11	4½	2.041
– Electric *(Torpedo nobiliana)*	69	0	20	9.072
– Homelyn *(Raja montagui)*	8.28		5	2.268
– Undulate *(Raja undulata)*	18		14	6.350
– Painted *(Raja microocellata)*	14.37		10	4.536
– Sting *(Dasyatis pastinaca)*	51		30	13.608
Ray's Bream *(Brama brama)*	6	4¼	5	2.268
Red Sea Bream *(Pagellus bogaraveo)*	9	6	4½	2.041
Rockling, Three Bearded *(Gaidropsarus vulgaris)*	3	1	1¾	.794
Scad *(Trachurus trachurus)*	1.97		1½	.680
Shad – Allis *(Alosa alosa)*	–		4	1.814
– Twaite *(Alosa fallax)*	2.87		2	.907
Shark – Porbeagle *(Lamna nasus)*	365	0	150	68.038
– Blue *(Prionace glauca)*	206	0	100	45.359
– Thresher *(Alopias vulpinus)*	–	–	120	54.431
– Mako *(Isurus oxyrinchus)*	–	–	200	90.718
– Six-Gilled *(Hexanchus griseus)*	154		100	45.359

Species			
Skate – Common (Raja batis)	221	0	suspended
– White (Raja alba)	165	0	120 54.431
– Long Nose (Raja oxyrinchus)	–	–	80 36.287
Smooth Hound (Mustelus asterias)	13.75		7 3.175
Stone Basse (Polyprion americanus)	10	13	8 3.628
Tope (Galeorhinus galeus)	66	8	40 18.144
Torsk (Brosme brosme)	4.7 kg		6 2.721
Trigger Fish (Balistes carolinensis)			3.25 1.474
Tunny (Thunnus thynnus)	–	–	100 45.359
Turbot (Scophthalmus maximus)	34	0	18 8.165
Whiting (Merlangus merlangus)	4	14½	3 1.361
Wrasse, Ballan (Labrus bergylta)	4.3 kg		4¾ 2.154
Wrasse, Cuckoo (Labrus mixtus)	1.94		1¼ .567

SOME NOTES ON TACKLE FOR USE WHILE SEA FISHING IN IRELAND

ROD	USE	REEL AND LINE
8–9 ft fibreglass or carbon spinning rod	Float fishing or spinning from harbour walls, piers or rocks for Mullet, Mackerel, Pollack, Coalfish and Bass.	Freshwater type fixed spool reel loaded with 4–10 lbs b.s. monofilament line.
9–10 ft fibreglass or carbon uptide boat casting rod	Boat fishing in shallow water bays for wide range of species from Dabs to Tope, or for shore fishing for some species such as Wrasse and Conger.	Medium sized casting multiplier or fixed spool reel loaded with 10–20 lbs b.s. monofilament.
7 or 8 ft fibreglass semicarbon or carbon boat rod up to 15–30 lbs. class	General boat fishing for Cod, Ling, Pollack, Ray and Tope.	Medium sized boat reel (4/0) loaded with 20-30 lbs b.s. monofilament or dacron line.
7 or 8 ft fibreglass or carbon boat rod up to 50 lbs. class.	Boat fishing for larger species such as Common Skate.	4/0–6/0 boat reel loaded with 30–50 lbs b.s. monofilament or dacron line.
11–12 ft carbon, semicarbon or fibreglass beach rod.	Shore fishing (where casting is necessary) from beaches, piers or rocks for all inshore species, including Flounder, Plaice, Ray, Codling and Bass.	Small to medium sized casting multiplier loaded with 15–18 lbs monofilament and having a shock leader of 40 lbs b.s. or over.

Louth, Meath & Dublin

Our sea angling tour starts at Carlingford Lough and the border between Co. Down in Northern Ireland and Co. Louth in the Republic. The Lough itself has fine scenery, with its backdrop of the Mourne Mountains on the northern shore and the Cooley Peninsula just to the south. It's very like a fiord running back into the highlands (though, in fact, it isn't one) and has strong tidal currents.

The rest of Louth consists of the shallow waters of Dundalk Bay, the rocky outcrop of Clogher Head and the north side of the Boyne estuary. After that comes the short coastline of Co. Meath, a very popular area with Dublin holiday-makers, particularly the sandy beaches of Bettystown and Laytown.

North Co. Dublin also has some popular holiday resorts, but probably offers better angling and has some important commercial fishing harbours. The estuaries at Rogerstown and Malahide hold some interest for the specimen hunter, but Dublin Bay itself is probably of most interest to the bait digger, with what may well be the best worm beds in the country.

This long stretch of coast gets surprisingly little angling pressure, considering how close it is to the main population centres of the country. Carlingford itself is mainly fished by Belfast anglers. It's mostly boat fishing in the shipping channel and it has produced the Irish record Tope. The Tope are still there, and so are good Ray and Cod in autumn. There is some shore fishing off cobble beaches around Greenore and a Tope from the shore should be possible though, to the best of my knowledge, this has never been done. Perhaps more Dublin anglers should look north instead of always heading for Wexford.

Dundalk Bay is also lightly fished, though it produces some Dogfish, Ray and Tope. The Boyne estuary is more interesting. Bass up to specimen size on sandeels free-lined from the shore are the main quarry, though Sea Trout and Flounder are also taken. There is some Mullet angling from the quays. The Boyne itself is of considerable interest to all-round anglers. It's slowly recovering from a fairly severe drainage scheme and anyone who wants a change from salt water will find excellent Brown Trout fishing, some Salmon and Sea Trout and some good coarse fishing in the lower reaches.

Clogher Head offers rock fishing into deep water, which is an unusual feature on the east coast, and some pier fishing at nearby Port Oriel – which goes to prove that the little-known stretch of coast covered by this chapter can provide every type of shore and dinghy fishing in Ireland.

North Co. Dublin has a special place in my mental album of fishing memories. It was in Balbriggan, many years ago, that Des Brennan introduced me to the fascinating business of Mullet fishing. The Mullet are still there, up to specimen size. You can stand on the end of the outer pier on a calm, sunny day a couple of hours before high tide and actually see them streaming in to glean the fish offal and prawn heads off the harbour bottom.

You fish a couple of hours each side of high water on a nice warm summer's day with fine coarse fishing tackle and a pinch of Mackerel on a size twelve hook. I was doing it once when I hooked a Mullet which gave me what I think is the longest run I've ever had from a fish of any species. It took a hundred and twenty yards of four-pound line off the Mitchell 300 before a trawler coming out of the harbour steamed across and broke me.

The estuaries of Rogerstown and Malahide are primarily the stalking grounds of the patient specimen hunter who is prepared to put in many days to catch a monster Bass. But this stretch of coast has other things to offer as well as being opened up by the rapidly growing fleet of dinghy anglers, attracted by the many slips, beaches and other launching facilities. The harbour at Skerries has a special claim to fame to the dinghy owner with an interest in wildlife – there is no place in the country where you will get a better chance to watch enormous Atlantic grey seals at close quarters.

Howth is primarily a boat angling centre, though there is rock fishing at Balscadden and the Baily. It is the closest harbour to the Kish Bank, which may not produce the amounts of Turbot it did in the past, but which still has plenty of Spurdog, Codling and Whiting in season.

Dublin Bay produces fish of a variety of species every year, but then it gets a lot of pressure. I reserve it for bait digging, though occasionally I slip a dinghy in at Bullock or Coliemore, where there are also small boats for hire, for a sunny afternoon of messing around the Muglins. Killiney Bay is also stronger on scenery than fish.

Before we leave Louth, Meath and Dublin, it's worth mentioning that there is accommodation all the way along the coast, though most anglers are on day trips. Tackle and bait are, of course, freely available from various shops in Dublin but can be hard to come by farther north. The Liffey estuary, like the Boyne estuary, offers some worthwhile coarse and game fishing.

Carlingford Lough, the Boyne estuary and much of North Co. Dublin certainly offer undeveloped fishing, particularly for the angler with a dinghy behind the car. There are several spots on the map which should be marked: 'Well worth exploring'.

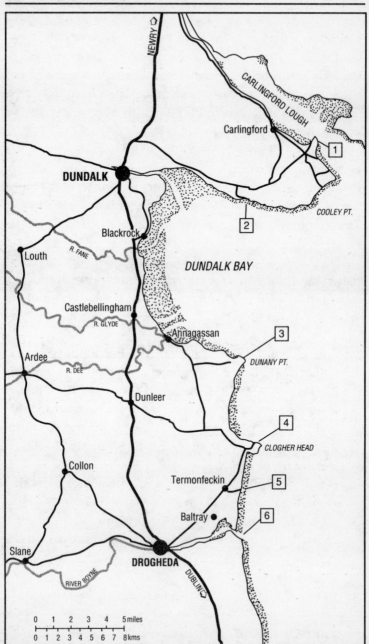

■ DESCRIPTION: LOUTH

The nine-mile-long east-facing Carlingford Lough forms a natural boundary between Co. Down in Northern Ireland and Co. Louth in the Republic. Inshore boat fishing is popular on the lough during the summer months, with Tope and Ray being the prime species on offer. The Irish Record Tope of 66½ lbs was caught there in 1979. Virtually every season throws up a number of specimens over 40 lbs.

As the coast swings south through Dundalk Bay, so the inshore waters become very shallow, broken only by Dunany Point and the large rocky promontory at Clogher Head where there is interesting and under-utilised shore fishing in summer. The inshore waters again become shallow to the south until the estuary of the River Boyne is reached.

The River Boyne is well known as a Salmon and Trout fishery, but the estuarine waters also hold a small localised population of Bass, many of which have exceeded the specimen size of 10 lbs.

■ SHORE ANGLING MARKS (map – page 29)

1. GREENORE: Below the lighthouse, spinning accounts for Mackerel, Sea Trout, Pollack and occasional Bass. Bottom fishing on slack tides in summer produces Spurdog, Ray and Dogfish. Wrasse close to the weed margins. During autumn and early winter, Codling can also be taken, particularly at night.
2. GYLES QUAY: Pier fishing at high water for Dabs, Flounder, Plaice and Dogfish. Conger at night.
3. DUNANY POINT: To the east of Annagassan, there is shore fishing for Codling, Flounder, Dabs, Coalfish and occasional Bass and Sea Trout. Fishes particularly well after an easterly blow.
4. CLOGHER HEAD: Pier and rock fishing for Dabs, Plaice, Mullet, Conger, Mackerel in season and Codling in winter.
5. TERMONFECKIN: Where the fresh water runs onto the beach is a hot spot for Flounder, Sea Trout and Dogfish.

Bass have also been taken there. Fishes well after an easterly wind.

6. RIVER BOYNE ESTUARY: Fishing from the Baltray side provides good sport for Bass, Flounder, Coalfish and occasional Sea Trout. Many specimen Bass (10 lbs+) have been taken here by spinning or freelining.

■ BAIT

Obtaining fresh bait is a major problem in this area and usually anglers must be prepared to carry a supply with them. There are, however, some lugworm beds below the Castletown River on Dundalk Bay.

■ APPROVED BOAT FOR HIRE

Boat Name	Queen Maeve
Skipper/Owner	Peadar Elmore, North Commons, Carlingford, Co. Louth
Base	Carlingford Harbour
Telephone	(042) 73239
Length	10.3 m (34 ft)
No. of Anglers	Bottom 6; Wreck 12
Facilities	Radio, Sounder, Navigator, Toilet, Washup, Cooking equipment
Daily Charter	£100 (minimum)
Daily Individual	£15
Weekly Charter	£400 (minimum)
Tackle Hire	Bottom outfit – £2 daily, £8 weekly. Bait supplied free.

■ NOTABLE CAPTURES

Species	Weight (lbs)	Location	Date
Bass	10.6	Baltray	8/89
Tope	62.5	Carlingford	6/89
Tope	55	Carlingford	6/89
Tope	56	Carlingford	6/90
Pollack	13	Carlingford	7/90
Spurdog	13	Dundalk Bay	8/91
Scad	1.55	Clogher Head	8/91
Pouting	3.19	Carlingford	9/91

IRISH RECORD

Species	Weight (lbs)	Location	Date
Tope	66 lbs 8 oz	Carlingford Lough	7/79

COMMON SPECIES

Common Species	Average Size Caught (lbs)
Tope	35 lbs
Ray	10 lbs
Dogfish	2 lbs
Bull Huss	10 lbs
Spurdog	9 lbs
Conger	15 lbs
Codling	4 lbs
Whiting	1 lb

TACKLE SHOPS

R.Q. O'Neill, Earl Street, Dundalk
Emerald Sports, Earl Street, Dundalk
Magee Sports, Shopping Centre, Dundalk
Olraine Agencies, Abbey Shopping Centre, West Street, Drogheda

CLUBS AND CONTACTS

No clubs listed at present.
Contact: Peadar Elmore, North Commons, Carlingford, Co. Louth (042) 73239.

COMPETITIONS

As no clubs are listed for this area, there are no organised competitions.

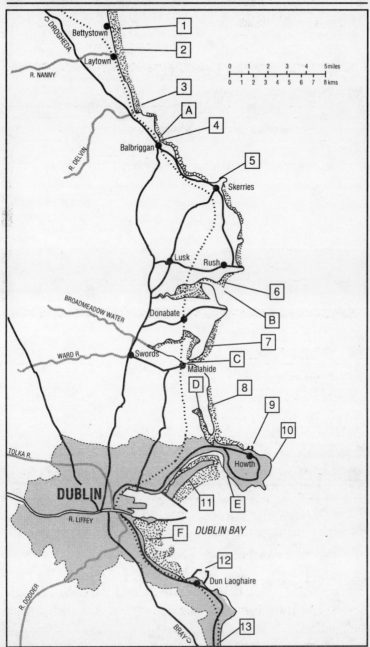

From Mornington on the southern side of the Boyne, the coast of Co. Meath runs for some seven miles to the mouth of the Delvin River at Gormanston. The beaches in this area are rather flat and featureless. But as the Co. Dublin coastline is reached, it becomes much more varied, with rocky outcrops and deeper water around Skerries. South of the village of Rush lie the large estuaries of Rogerstown and Malahide and the smaller inlet at Baldoyle. All excellent bait gathering areas.

The deep-water harbour at Howth is sheltered to the south-east by the large outcrop of Howth Head which reaches 500 feet at its highest point and also forms the northern extremity of Dublin Bay which drains the Tolka, Liffey and Dodder rivers and the Royal and Grand canals.

The southern side of Dublin Bay and the ferry port of Dun Laoghaire are backed by the high ground of Dalkey Point before the coast turns south again through the picturesque Killiney Bay to the River Dargle, which is the southern boundary of Co. Dublin.

The capital city and its environs boast the largest number of sea anglers in the country and no less than thirty-two clubs are listed for the area by the Irish Federation of Sea Anglers.

Boat fishing is carried out mainly from May to September, while shore fishing enthusiasts will find fair sport through to December.

■ SHORE ANGLING MARKS (map – see page 33)

1. BETTYSTOWN: The shallow beach offers occasional Bass, Sea Trout and Flounder. The most productive period is while the water is coloured after an easterly gale and surf conditions are prevalent.

2. LAYTOWN: Where the River Nanny flows into the sea at Laytown, there is some beach fishing for Bass, Sea Trout and Flounder. Evening tides are generally more productive. Mullet are known to have taken flies intended for Sea Trout in the pool below the railway bridge.

3. GORMANSTON: Occasional Bass and Flatfish can be taken while beach fishing during the summer months at the Delvin River mouth below Gormanston. As in the previous venues, this section of beach fishes best on evening tides during or immediately after an easterly blow. The most popular baits are ragworm, lugworm and peeler crab, but when a surf is running, ledgered sandeel can be the most successful.

4. BALBRIGGAN: Some of the best Mullet fishing on the east coast can be had in the tidal habour at Balbriggan. The Mullet there move in and out with the tide and the optimum time for fishing is two hours either side of high water. A small commercial fishing fleet is based at Balbriggan and the Mullet are conditioned to feeding on fish offal washed from the trawlers. Pieces of fish are therefore by far the best baits to use in this situation and they should either be freelined or float fished.

Flounder can be taken during daylight while fishing over the sand at the back of the pier and autumn produces Whiting at night.

5. SKERRIES: Small Pollack and Mackerel can be caught while spinning at high water from the pier at Skerries, where Flatfish are also common over the sand. Mullet can also be taken at times by float fishing or freelining small pieces of fish flesh. A number of specimen Mullet (5 lbs+) have been taken in recent years.

6. ROGERSTOWN ESTUARY: Freelined sandeel in the main channel during spring and autumn can be productive for Bass and occasional Sea Trout. Spinning can also be very effective, particularly on a flooding tide. In surf conditions, Bass and Flounder can be taken from the main beach; autumn best. Specimen fish have been recorded.

7. DONABATE: Night fishing in autumn turns up occasional Codling, Bass and Flatfish. The areas just south of the Martello Tower and opposite the lifeguard's hut are the hotspots. Bass can also be taken in autumn at the mouth of

Malahide Estuary, with a flood tide being the optimum period. Specimen Flounder and Bass have been taken in this area.

8. VELVET STRAND: Below the championship golf course at Portmarnock, the beach produces Flounder, Dab and Plaice. The area around the rocks is regarded as the prime location, particularly at night. Bass have also been recorded in spring and autumn. Distance casting during these periods will also produce Dogfish, Codling and Whiting.

9. HOWTH: This busy harbour has experienced vast development in recent years. In summer literally hundreds of anglers visit the venue for Mackerel fishing. Pollack, Codling, Whiting and Mullet are also available.

10. HOWTH HEAD: During the summer, angling places are eagerly sought on the northern shore of Howth Head at Balscadden where a wide variety of fish can be taken, including Mackerel, Plaice, Dabs, Dogfish, Pouting, Whiting and Codling.

    To the north of the Baily lighthouse there is restricted access to rock fishing for Coalfish, Codling, Dabs, Plaice and Dogfish. The rough ground at Red Rock close to the dinghy club produces Bass to specimen size, Flounder and occasional Dogfish.

11. DOLLYMOUNT STRAND: This beach which fronts Bull Island is a popular bathing place for 'Northside' Dubliners. Evening tides in mid summer and autumn can be productive for Bass, Flounder, freshwater Eels and Codling. The best bass recorded was taken in September 1985 and weighed 13.25 lbs.

12. DUN LAOGHAIRE: The harbour provides pier fishing for much of the year. From the West Pier, Dabs, Conger, Bass and Plaice to specimen size have been recorded. Whiting, Codling, Pouting and Coalfish can also be taken from the pier head in autumn. On the seaward side of the West Pier, spinning over rough ground accounts for Mackerel and Pollack from July to September.

13. KILLINEY BAY: South of Sorrento Point lies this very picturesque beach. There is sporadic shore fishing for Plaice, Dogfish and occasional Bass. Recent summers have seen a good run of Codling with evening tides being most productive.

■ BAIT (map – page 33)

A. BALBRIGGAN: Lugworm can be dug on the beach north of the harbour. Peeler crab are common beneath the outer pier wall.

B. ROGERSTOWN ESTUARY: Lugworm are plentiful on the mudflats, while sandeel can occasionally be taken from the outer banks at low water.

C. MALAHIDE ESTUARY: A prime bait gathering location and the Corballis area to the north has extensive lugworm beds. Ragworm, mussel, clam and cockles can also be collected locally.

D. BALDOYLE CREEK: Lugworm and ragworm are available in the mudflats opposite the church.

E. RED ROCK: Crab around the rocks at low water. Lugworm, clam and some white ragworm in sandy patches, particularly below dinghy club. Ragworm on mussel banks to east.

F. SANDYMOUNT: Black lugworm and occasional clam below promenade and at Cockle Lake near power station. Some white ragworm at Dun Laoghaire side of bay near windsurfing school.

■ NOTABLE CAPTURES

Species	Weight (lbs)	Location	Bait	Boat/Shore	Date
Bass	10.53	Portrane	Ragworm	S	8/89
Bass	11.00	Malahide	Sandeel	S	9/90
Bass	11.48	Donabate	Ragworm	S	9/88
Bass	11.50	Laytown	Ragworm	S	10/90

Species	Weight (lbs)	Location	Bait	Boat/Shore	Date
Bass	11.87	Corballis	Ragworm	S	8/89
Bass	12.00	Dollymount	Rag/ Lug cocktail	S	9/88
Bass	12.35	Dun Laoghaire	Mackerel/ Rag cocktail	S	9/87
Dab	1.5	Kish Bank	Lugworm	B	9/88
Dogfish (L.S.D.)	3.87	Howth	Mackerel	B	9/91
Pollack	13.62	Kish Bank	Pirk	B	9/88
Spurdog	17.20	Lambay	Mackerel	B	7/87
Spurdog	17.00	Kish Bank	Mackerel	B	8/87
Dogfish (G.S.D.)	16.00	Rush	Mackerel	B	9/91
Smooth Hound	7.00	Howth	Ragworm	S	7/90
Tope	52.50	Rush	Mackerel	B	8/90
Grey Mullet	5.75	Balbriggan	Herring	S	9/91
Grey Mullet	5.56	Skerries	Mackerel	S	8/91

◼ COMMON SPECIES

Common Species	Average Size Caught (lbs)
Bass	4
Cod	2
Coalfish	1
Conger	10
Dab	.5
Lesser Spotted Dogfish	2
Flounder	1.5
Mackerel	.75
Spurdog	8
Greater Spotted Dogfish	8
Thornback Ray	8
Tope	25
Whiting	1

■ TACKLE SHOPS

ABC Angling Requirements, 15 St Mary's Abbey, Dublin 7,
(01) 731525

Angling and Sports Centre, 13 Main Street, Blackrock,
Co. Dublin, (01) 288 7086

Patrick Cleere and Son Ltd, 5 Bedford Row, Dublin 2, (01) 777406

Michael Dixon Tackle, 36 Ralahine, Ballybrack, Co. Dublin,
(01) 285 4159

Dun Laoghaire Angling, 129 Lower Georges Street,
Dun Laoghaire, (01) 284 2462

Gaynestown, Main Street, Blanchardstown, Dublin 15,
(01) 201127

Henry's Tackle Shop, 19 Ballybough Road, Dublin 3,
(01) 745691

Nolan's, 80 North Strand, Dublin 3, (01) 744520

Rory's, 17a Temple Bar, Dublin 2, (01) 772351

Southside Angling, 43 Upper Clanbrassil Street, Dublin 8,
(01) 530266

Watts Bros, 18 Upper Ormond Quay, Dublin 7, (01) 778574

Johnnie Watts, 163 Mobhi Road, Glasnevin, Dublin 9,
(01) 370310

■ CLUBS AND CONTACTS

There are too many clubs in Meath and Dublin to list here. Further
details can be obtained from IFSA Leinster Secretary, Frank
Baxter, 20a Spencer Street, North Strand, Dublin 3, (01) 747263.

For enquiries on Match fishing and Tournament Casting,
contact: Irish Match Angling and Surf-casting Association,
Secretary Paul Keegan, 80 Moreen Avenue, Sandyford,
Dublin 16, (01) 952157.

■ COMPETITIONS

There are generally several friendly boat competitions in the
area every year, but no official events are listed.

Bray to Courtown

INTRODUCTION

In comparison with the last chapter, this one is a very different kettle of fish. It is a bit low on scenery, but certainly high on angling pressure. It provides some excellent beach fishing on winter nights. Dinghy fishing, which peaked in the seventies, shows some signs of coming back again in recent years.

The stretch of coast from Greystones to Wicklow town has been described recently by a foreign commentator as 'probably the best match stretch in Europe'. This, of course, doesn't mean the best angling in Europe. It means long, even stretches of steep beach with good access and a fair distribution of fish.

Bray itself and Bray Head provide a bit of angling, but it isn't until you get to Greystones that the interest really starts. The North Beach is probably for less serious fishing while the kids kick a football. I remember fishing a 'fun' competition on it once which I nearly won by digging some minute coarse fishing hooks out of my tackle bag, tipping them with white rag and running up to the steward every few minutes with Flounders, Coalies, Codling and Sea Scorpions, the largest of which wasn't over six inches long.

Greystones is a very important centre for dinghy angling and club boats from Dublin clubs. If you take a dinghy out over the offshore sand-banks yourself, remember that tides

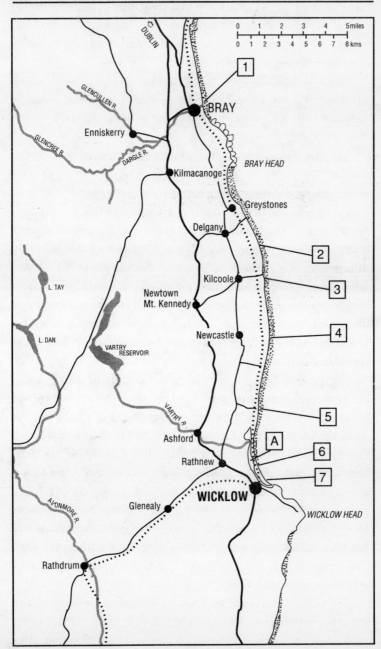

along this coast are powerful and a little erratic. When the tide turns against the wind, an evil and dangerous chop can get up very rapidly. The compensation can be excellent fishing for a variety of species from Tope to Dabs, with some particularly fine Plaice to be got on mussel bait.

South Beach, Greystones, is the start of the famous match stretch, but not the most popular part of it. At times it can be excellent, but all too often it lives up to its nickname of 'The Hungry Acre'.

All the way down to Wicklow town, the beach is very similar. The cream of the fishing is for Codling on night tides in autumn and winter. Long casting is often a help and this, of course, demands heavy tackle. A two pound fish would be a good one and, personally, I'm not crazy about using five ounce leads and forty pound shock leaders for fish of this size. But different strokes... The problems are compounded after a blow, when there's often a lot of floating weed.

Despite the fact that this match stretch is very fair and even, there are certain hot-spots and holes which devotees swear by. The detailed text of the chapter and the maps will point you in the right direction.

The pleasure angler should note a couple of things about big matches – and this stretch of coast often sees up to two hundred British and Irish anglers battling it out over several days for hefty prizes. First of all, the disturbance of all that terminal tackle continually crashing out a hundred and fifty yards begins to annoy the fish after a while. So while this is going on, it can be quite a good idea to set up quietly half a mile below the match and pick up the Codling that are looking for a bit of peace. Secondly, quite enormous amounts of bait get thrown into the sea at these matches. So when they are over, there is rich picking for several days for the fish – and the enterprising pleasure angler.

The coast from Wicklow town to Arklow offers more varied scenery, but less consistent fishing.

The whole stretch of coast from Bray down has a number of local clubs, but it is really the major fishing grounds for the Dublin-based clubs and this is where a lot of the expertise about shore and boat marks lies. It would be a good idea for an angler new to this area to join one of these bigger Dublin clubs.

Wicklow can provide some very fine sea angling, but is rather less attractive to the all-round angler who likes to vary his sport by wetting a line in fresh water from time to time. There is virtually no coarse angling in the east of the county and, though some of the coastal rivers have sporadic runs of Sea Trout and Grilse, it requires a lot of local knowledge to be in the right place at the right time. The acid geology of the county also means that Brown Trout are plentiful in the faster reaches of the rivers and streams, but they have a poor average size.

My own view of shore angling along this coast is that it is undoubtedly a matchman's paradise. But the pleasure angler should be selective, fishing it when the Codling are in or when there are other good runs of fish, but heading farther north or south during the lean times. Boat and dinghy fishing is more consistent and, weather permitting, can provide some interest in every month of the year.

■ DESCRIPTION: BRAY HEAD TO WICKLOW HEAD

The fifteen mile (24 km) stretch of coast between Bray Head and Wicklow Head is one of the most popular shore fishing areas in Ireland. The steep-to beaches north and south of Greystones and at Kilcoole, Newcastle, Killoughter and North Beach, Wicklow are used extensively for shore competitions.

The offshore mussel banks and sandbars are also popular with inshore boat enthusiasts.

All the beaches in this region are capable of producing Codling for much of the year, with the period from September to late January usually most productive.

Summer fishing for Plaice and Ray can also be excellent from dinghies, with the area between Newcastle and Wicklow Head particularly interesting.

■ SHORE ANGLING MARKS (map – page 41)

Caution: Care should be taken while crossing railway tracks.

1. BRAY: Pier fishing for Codling, Pollack, Dogfish and occasional Conger. Beach fishing below promenade for Bass, Plaice, Flounder and Codling.
2. SOUTH BEACH, GREYSTONES: Beach fishing for Codling, Pollack, Coalfish, Plaice, Dab, Dogfish, Flounder and occasional Ray and Bass.
3. KILCOOLE: Beach fishing for Codling, Pollack, Flounder, Coalfish, Plaice, Dab, Dogfish and occasional Bass, Ray and Whiting. Autumn best.
4. NEWCASTLE: Beach fishing for Codling (especially at railway worker's hut), Coalfish, Dab and occasional Conger, Bass and Gurnard. High water best.
5. KILLOUGHTER: Beach fishing for Codling, Dab and occasional Ray and Bass. Night fishing.
6. NORTH BEACH, WICKLOW: Beach fishing for Codling, Dogfish, Dab, small Plaice, Coalfish and occasional Bass. Flood tide best.
7. WICKLOW: Pier fishing for Flounder (inside harbour), Dogfish, Dab and occasional small Ray.

■ BAIT (map – page 41)

A. BROADLOUGH/WICKLOW HARBOUR: Some lugworm available in harbour area and upper reaches of Broadlough. Spring tide lows most productive.

Bait is usually impossible to obtain in this area, owing to exposed nature of coastline. The nearest available worm beds are in Dublin Bay.

APPROVED BOATS FOR HIRE

There are no approved charter boats operating in this area. However, there are boat-launching slips at Bray Harbour, Greystones Harbour and Wicklow Harbour.

NOTABLE CAPTURES

Species	Weight (lbs)	Location	Bait	Boat/Shore	Date
Bass	11.35	Greystones	Mackerel	S	11/89
Bass	10.01	Greystones	Mussel	S	10/89
Black sole	2.39	Wicklow	Ragworm	S	9/89
Bull Huss	17.44	Wicklow	Mackerel	B	8/89
Bull Huss	16.38	Wicklow	Mackerel	B	8/89
Thornback Ray	25.00	Greystones	Mackerel	B	5/89
Thornback Ray	22.00	Greystones	Mackerel	B	5/89
Tope	43.50	Wicklow	Mackerel	B	8/89
Tope	42.50	Greystones	Mackerel	B	8/89
Tope	40.50	Kilcoole	Mackerel	B	7/89
Tope	57.50	Greystones	Mackerel	B	8/91
Bass	11.40	Greystones	Mackerel	S	9/90
Blonde Ray	27.50	Greystones	Mackerel	B	9/90
Smooth Hound	10.00	Five Mile Pt.	Crab	S	6/91

IRISH RECORD

Smooth Hound	13.75 lbs	Five Mile Point, Wicklow	Crab	S	6/91

COMMON SPECIES

Common Species	Average Size Caught (lbs)
Cod	2.5
Plaice	2
Dogfish	2
Pollack	3.5
Coalfish	1.5
Dabs	0.5
Thornback Ray	11
Blonde Ray	15
Tope	25
Spurdog	6

■ TACKLE SHOPS

Bray Sports, 21 Main Street, Bray
The Sports Shop, High Street, Wicklow
Dargle Tackle, 5 Everett Centre, Castle Street, Bray,
(01) 286 9215

■ CLUBS AND CONTACTS

Bray Sea Anglers, H. Gilbert, Ledwidge Crescent, Bray
Co. Wicklow
Greystones Ridge SAC, N. Brown, 48 Seaview, Kilcoole,
Co. Wicklow, (0404) 895683 (Work)
John Paul (1979) SAC, M. Fortune, 5 Benners Parade, Bray,
Co. Wicklow, (01) 282 1149
Scorpion SAC, B. Brierton, Flat 9, 5 Prince of Wales Terrace,
Bray, Co. Wicklow, (01) 286 9215 (Work)
Wicklow Bay SAC (Rural), P. Flahive, 24 Woodside, Rathnew,
Co. Wicklow
Wicklow Bay SAC, J. Byrne, 24 Seafield Road, Wicklow,
(0404) 67716

■ COMPETITIONS

The Wicklow beaches are used extensively for shore matches. During the summer, and for much of the winter months, hardly a weekend goes by without some sort of event being staged.

The East Coast International takes place every January when large numbers of UK visitors compete. Other major events include the Leinster Open, which can attract over 300 competitors annually.

Small boat fishing events are also staged throughout the summer from Greystones or Wicklow. These events are always well supported.

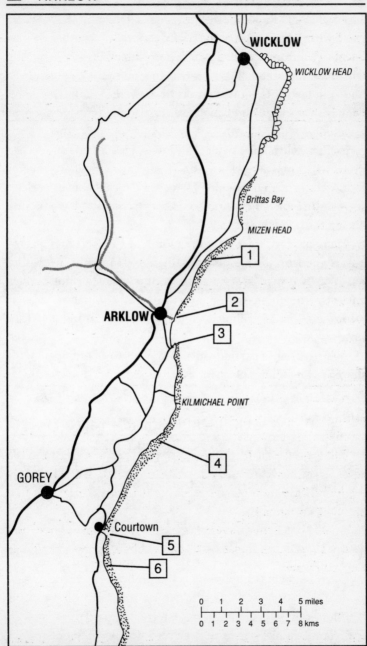

■ DESCRIPTION: WICKLOW HEAD TO COURTOWN

South of Wicklow Head, the coastline is generally shallow and sandy, broken in places by rocky outcrops. The beaches at Silver Strand and Brittas Bay are popular bathing locations which attract large holiday crowds in summer. It is possible to find quieter spots, however, and below the quaintly named Pennycomequick Bridge, there is access to the pleasant shore at Ennereilly.

Farther south, the town of Arklow stands astride the Avoca River which enters the sea at a small harbour where several commercial trawlers operate. Here, some local boats offer deep sea angling on an ad hoc basis, particularly at weekends during the holiday season.

There are breakwaters at the mouth of the river and a large pier owned by the Cement Roadstone Company lies to the south of the town. There are also a number of secluded coves and strands in this area, particularly on either side of Kilmichael Point at Kilmichael Strand, Clones Strand and Tara Cove.

Boat fishing is carried out from May to September, with shore angling taking place for much of the year.

■ SHORE ANGLING MARKS (map – page 47)

1. PENNYCOMEQUICK/ENNEREILLY: Beach fishing near streams for Bass, Flounder, Whiting, Codling, Dogfish and Plaice. Fishes best in winter at night.
2. SOUTH BEACH: Bass, Codling, Dabs, Flounder. Specimen Black Sole recorded. Best fished by night.
3. ROADSTONE PIER: Bottom fishing for Codling, Dabs, Plaice, Whiting, Dogfish, Flounder and Pouting. Permission to fish this jetty is required.
4. CLONES STRAND: Beach fishing for Codling, Bass and Flounder, especially after easterly winds. Tope, Smooth Hound and Ray have all been recorded in summer.

5. COURTOWN: Mullet fishing in harbour, high tide best. Beach fishing for Bass, Flounder, Dogfish and occasional Smooth Hound and Ray. Specimen Bass recorded here.
6. POLLSHORE: Beach fishing for Bass, Flounder, Dogfish, Pouting and Codling. Night tides best. Spinning from rocks at Roney Point for Bass.

■ BAIT

Bait is impossible to come by in this area, so anglers must be prepared to bring it with them.

■ APPROVED BOATS FOR HIRE

There are no approved boats for hire in this area, but commercial trawlers may take out anglers occasionally at weekends from Arklow, and a part-time angling boat is based at Courtown.

■ NOTABLE CAPTURES

Species	Weight (lbs)	Location	Bait	Boat/Shore	Date
Conger	45.5	Courtown Hbr.	Mackerel	S	6/89
Freshwater Eel	3.00	Arklow	Ragworm	S	8/90
Rockling	1.98	Arklow	Mackerel	S	8/90
Smooth Hound	9.22	Kilmichael	Crab	S	7/91
Smooth Hound	7.93	Arklow	Crab	S	7/91

■ IRISH RECORD

Three Bearded Rockling   3 lbs 1 oz   Maurice Laurent   11/5/90   Arklow

COMMON SPECIES

Common Species	Average Size Caught (lbs)
Bass	4
Cod	2
Dab	.75
Lesser Spotted Dogfish	2
Flounder	1.5
Whiting	.75
Rockling	.75

TACKLE SHOPS

George O'Toole, Lower Main Street, Arklow
John Webb, 100 Main Street, Gorey

CLUBS AND CONTACTS

No local club at present in this area.

COMPETITIONS

Until recently, there were very few competitions staged in this area. However, Clones Strand has become a popular match venue and a number of events are staged there annually.

Cahore, Wexford & Hook Peninsula

INTRODUCTION

This chapter brings us to Wexford, one of the jewels in the crown of Irish sea angling. It is a county with great strands, sinuous estuaries, rock marks, superb dinghy fishing and some deep sea operators. There is also varied scenery, the best climate in Ireland and a good support structure of accommodation, bait and tackle.

Cahore is probably the most popular dinghy angling centre in the whole country. It's all 'tow-your-own', but the little slip can get quite busy in summer. What is attracting the attention is quality fishing for Tope, Spurs, Smoothies and Ray. There is also fishing for shoaling Bass, which seem to be making a bit of a comeback. In fact, Wexford generally offers the best consistent Bass fishing in the country at present since commercial pressure has thinned out numbers so dramatically in the south-west. There should be no need to remind genuine anglers that killing undersize Bass or taking too many full grown ones is not only un-sporting; it's also against the law.

A little farther south, around Kilmuckridge, is probably the real centre for Bass enthusiasts. But bear in mind that, by Irish standards, the coast around here gets a lot of angling pressure for the 'animals' in summer and the Bass in spring and autumn.

If Kilmuckridge has become the Bass capital of Ireland, Morriscastle and nearby Tinnabearna must be the Smooth Hound capitals. The list of specimens from this area is a long one, and it is also a popular match venue. But it must be mentioned that the Smooth Hound fishing has declined over the past couple of seasons, just as the Bass have improved.

The fishing on down to Wexford is a bit patchy, though worth exploration by the Bass angler. The harbour itself brings us to another species, the Flounder. I used to make a regular annual pilgrimage in October or November to fish the strands and creeks of the harbour for these mud-loving flatties. The fact that I haven't done it for the past couple of years is reminding me how much I miss it. This year for sure!

Rosslare is probably emerging as the big new venue on the east coast. It really all started when parties of English and Welsh anglers began using the car ferry which docks there to bring over dinghies on trailers. Their explorations of inshore marks around Rosslare and round to the Saltee Islands, plus the shore fishing they did when it got choppy, produced such phenomenal results in terms of quality and variety that Irish anglers woke up to the potential of this bottom corner of the country. The English anglers come back every year for an autumn festival which is dominated by Pollack, Cod and Ray but which has produced no less that twenty-eight different species recently.

The nearby Splaugh Rock was a legendary Bass mark in the sixties. Commercial pressure killed that off, but now and again it splutters into life and trolled Red-gills produce marvellous angling. The rocky ground around the Saltees produces quality Pollack and Wrasse, as well as Tope. Kilmore Quay is the logical place to launch a boat, and informal chartering is usually possible.

Along Wexford's south coast, Ballyteigue has produced the last two Irish record Flounder. No better place if you're looking for a specimen, though the next big bay to the east, Bannow Bay, can be almost as good. Autumn and winter are the times when the Flounder specimen hunters congregate. My information is that some of these Flounder specialists are catching more big Bass than they're letting on about.

That brings us along to the rocky peninsula tipped by Hook Head. It offers the first area since this tour started in Co. Louth where there is a wide choice of rock marks for the angler who specialises in this type of fishing. The angler who may be trying it for the first time should remember how dangerous rock marks can be and how many sea anglers have lost their lives to those sinister 'freak waves'.

The Hook is a nice area to spend an angling holiday. It doesn't just have rock marks. There is beach fishing, the whole of Waterford Harbour on the west side of the peninsula to explore, and the Flounder and Bass marks to the east. There are dinghy launching facilities and a particularly good back-up of tourist information, accommodation of various kinds and just about everything except sharks. And maybe they're there if anyone tried hard enough.

Wexford has all this, and even some good fishing for the game angler. The Slaney, which hits the sea in Wexford Harbour, is the top Salmon river on the east coast these days. The Salmon fishing is concentrated in March, April and a bit of May, but there can be quite good fishing for small Sea Trout after that in early summer.

There's no doubt about it, Wexford is great. If you haven't fished there, don't leave it too long. Ideally, hitch a dinghy behind the car, stick a bait fork in the boot, lash rods for all types of fishing to the roof, and head off for a week... or two... or three.

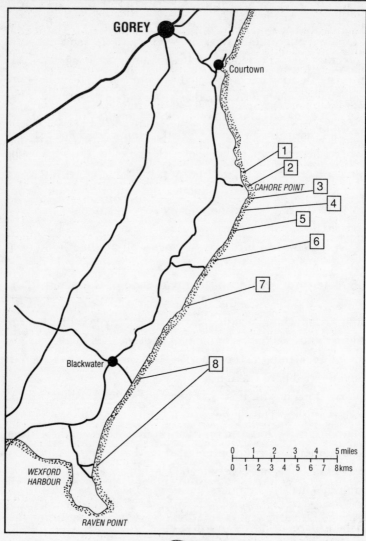

GOREY

Courtown

1

2

CAHORE POINT 3

4

5

6

7

8

Blackwater

WEXFORD
HARBOUR

RAVEN POINT

0   1   2   3   4   5 miles
0 1 2 3 4 5 6 7 8 kms

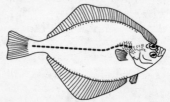

DESCRIPTION: CAHORE

In the last ten years, the small north Wexford village of Cahore has become synonymous with some of the best inshore boat and shore fishing on the east coast. A wide variety of species has been recorded recently and in 1988 the Irish Specimen Fish Committee received more specimen claims from this area than for any other sea angling centre in the country.

Generally boat fishing is over the sand banks which lie fairly close inshore, while shore angling is mainly concentrated on the shallow beaches to the south of Cahore Point.

Much is still to be learned about the fishing locally, but it has been established that the first run of summer species occurs during May when boat anglers will encounter Ray, Bull Huss, Tope, and Smooth Hound. By the time June comes along, beach anglers are finding fish – mainly at night.

SHORE ANGLING MARKS (map – page 54)

1. NORTH BEACH, CAHORE: Fishing between the groynes in the winter months for Codling, Whiting and Dabs. In summer for Flounder, Dogfish and Bass. Night tides best.

2. CAHORE PIER: Bottom fishing for Smooth Hound, Dogfish and Dabs in spring. Codling and Whiting in winter.

3. CAHORE POINT: Several rocky outcrops which give access to fairly deep water, over sand. The best area is immediately behind the castle. Fishing for Dabs, Plaice and occasional Bass. Dogfish can, however, be a nuisance at times.

4. BALLINOULART: Seldom fished until recently. Has proven productive for Bass (in surf conditions), Flounder and Dabs, Smooth Hound and occasional Ray in springtime.

5. MORRISCASTLE: One of the most popular of all east coast shore angling venues, extensively used for competitions. Many specimen fish have been recorded over the years from a wide range of species, including Monkfish, Painted Ray, Sting Ray, Smooth Hound, Bass, Bull Huss, Spurdog, Dogfish, Flounder, Dab and Tope.

6. TINNABEARNA: Unheard of ten years ago, but since the discovery of Smooth Hound locally has become a very popular springtime venue. Excellent fishing for Ray, Tope and Bass has also been experienced.

7. BALLINAMONA: Another popular beach, used widely for competitions. Produces Bass for much of the year, but tends to fish best in spring and early summer for Smooth Hound, Dogfish and Ray.

8. BLACKWATER/CURRACLOE: Beach fishing for Bass in spring and autumn. Flounders, Eels, Codling, Dogfish, Bull Huss and occasional Ray, Smooth Hound and Tope. Popular bathing places in summer, so night fishing is advised.

■ BAIT

There is no bait available locally.

The nearest venue where lugworm and clam can be obtained is in Wexford Harbour – below the municipal caravan park. Crab can also be collected in the weed margins.

Ragworm and frozen mackerel can occasionally be purchased from the general merchants in Ballygarrett.

■ APPROVED BOATS FOR HIRE

There are no deep sea angling boats at present in this area. However, small inshore boats may occasionally be organised through Club Secretary Ian Bottomley, Wayside Cottage, Cahore, (055) 27453.

■ NOTABLE CAPTURES

Species	Weight (lbs)	Location	Bait	Boat/Shore	Date
Bull Huss	18.30	Cahore	Mackerel	B	5/88
Bull Huss	17.00	Cahore	Mackerel	B	6/89
Grey Gurnard	2.00	Cahore	Mackerel	B	9/87
Spurdog	13.50	Cahore	Mackerel	B	6/89
Bass	10.53	Morriscastle	Rag/Squid	S	6/91
Painted Ray	10.90	Cahore	Mackerel	B	7/89

Species	Weight (lbs)	Location	Bait	Boat/Shore	Date
Thornback Ray	21.50	Cahore	Mackerel	B	6/91
Thornback Ray	22.00	Cahore	Mackerel	B	8/87
Homelyn Ray	5.13	Cahore	Herring	B	7/88
Tope	57.50	Cahore	Mackerel	B	6/91
Smooth Hound	10.67	Tinnabearna	Peeler Crab	S	6/85
Smooth Hound	9.70	Cahore	Peeler Crab	B	5/91

■ COMMON SPECIES

Common Species	Average Size Caught (lbs)
Bass	6
Cod	4
Dab	.75
Spurdog	8
Lesser Spotted Dogfish	2.5
Greater Spotted Dogfish	10
Flounder	1.5
Grey Gurnard	.75
Thornback Ray	10
Homelyn Ray	4
Painted Ray	6
Smooth Hound	4
Tope	35
Whiting	.75

■ TACKLE SHOPS

Some items of tackle and frozen bait can be obtained from The General Store, Ballygarrett.

■ CLUBS AND CONTACTS

Cahore SAC, A. Doyle, 117 Mount Tallant Avenue, Terenure, Dublin 6, (01) 903311.

Kilmuckridge SAC, M. Managan, Kilmuckridge, Gorey, Co. Wexford, (053) 30113.

Cahore, Ian Bottomley, Wayside Cottage, Cahore, (055) 27453.

■ COMPETITIONS

Several shore and boat competitions are organised in the area every year, mainly by the local clubs. Recently, several other clubs and organisations have also staged tournaments locally.

■ DESCRIPTION: SOUTH WEXFORD

The estuary of the River Slaney enters the sea in the sheltered Wexford Harbour. The town of Wexford lies on the southern shore and is ideally placed to cater for anglers. Shore match fishing is common in the harbour area and attracts large numbers of competitors throughout the summer.

Dinghy fishing is becoming very popular in the east Wexford area, particularly at Rosslare. However little deep sea angling is carried out, except from the tidal harbour at Carne. The main attraction there is the excellent boat fishing (in fine weather) at the Tuskar Rock.

During the summer, Wexford Harbour holds large numbers of immature Bass. These fish are below the legal size limit and should be returned safely to the water. Generally fishing begins around May and lasts through to November.

On the south Wexford coast, boat fishing from Kilmore Quay and Fethard-on-Sea is generally over mixed ground in depths of around 10 fathoms. A good variety of fish is available, especially off Hook Head and around the Saltee Islands. Recently dinghy angling has become extremely popular out of Kilmore. A new charter boat began operations in 1992 from Wexford Harbour.

Shore angling is quite popular in the area and many competitions are organised from the beaches at the Coombe and Burrow and the rock marks on the Hook. Flounder and Bass are

CAHORE, WEXFORD & HOOK PENINSULA

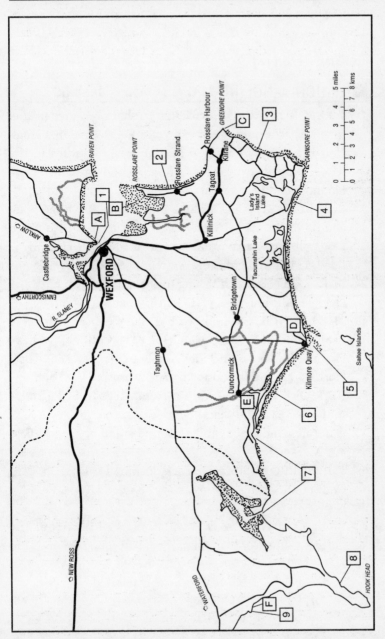

the most common species from the beaches, while Dogfish, Wrasse, Pollack and Conger are the main species from the rocks.

The season for boat fishing is generally June to September, while shore fishing is almost a year-round activity, February and March excepted.

■ SHORE ANGLING MARKS (map – page 59)

1. WEXFORD HARBOUR: Sheltered, shallow water fishing for Bass, Flounder and freshwater Eel. Occasional small Codling at new bridge. Popular match venues in the harbour are at Ardcavan and Katts Strand. Specimen Bass, Flounder and Eel recorded.

2. ROSSLARE STRAND: Fishing into channel from the point and on the beach between the groynes for Bass, Flounder, Dogfish and occasional Ray and Smooth Hound. A flooding tide at night is the optimum period.

3. BALLYTRENT: Beach fishing for Bass, Dabs, Flounder and Dogfish. Autumn best, particularly when surf is running.

4. THE COOMBE: Steep-to beach of shingle and sand. Shore fishing into fairly deep water for Bass, Codling, Dogfish, Flounder and occasional Ray, Sea Trout, Mackerel and Tope. Hotspots are at Rostoonstown and Tacumshin Lake outflow.

5. KILMORE QUAY: Spinning from rocks at St Patrick's Bridge for Bass and Mackerel in season. Pier fishing at high water in summer for Mullet, Flounder and occasional Bass and Mackerel.

6. THE BURROW: Steep-to beach. Fishing for Dogfish, Bass, Codling, Rockling and occasional Ray and Tope. Summer best.

7. BALLYTEIGUE AND BANNOW: Fishing from the northern shores of both estuaries and at estuary mouths for Flounder and Bass. Specimens of both species recorded. Occasional Sea Trout have been encountered.

8. HOOK HEAD: Rock fishing from various access points for Conger, Wrasse, Pollack, Coalfish, Dogfish and Rockling. Bass and Flatfish in sandy patches (Lumsdins Bay, Booley

Bay etc). This is a popular match fishing venue and rocks are numbered for competitions.

9. DUNCANNON: Bass, Flatfish and freshwater Eel, occasional Codling and Dogfish (bottom fishing) from strand. Spinning for Sea Trout in channel at low water. Conger from outer wall of harbour, below fort.

■ BAIT (map – page 59)

A. BELOW MUNICIPAL CAR PARK: Lugworm, ragworm and clam can be dug on the beach. Crab can be gathered in weed below Caravan Park.

B. SOUTH SLOB: Lugworm and ragworm can be dug and mussel gathered. A small boat is required to reach some of the more productive areas.

C. GREENORE POINT: Some lugworm and white ragworm between point and Meteorological Station.

D. KILMORE QUAY: Quality lugworm in harbour. Care should be taken while digging to avoid boat moorings.

E. BALLYTEIGUE LOUGH: Crab in weedy margins of northern shore. Lugworm on channel banks.

F. DUNCANNON: Lugworm on beach; southern section most productive.

■ APPROVED BOAT FOR HIRE

Boat Name	Aquastar
Skipper/Owner	Nicholas Bowie, 143 The Faythe, Wexford
Base	Wexford Harbour
Telephone	(053) 45888
Length	10 m (33 ft)
No. of Anglers	12
Facilities	Radio, Sounder, Radar, Navigator, Cooking equipment Toilet, Washup
Daily Charter	£160 (minimum)
Daily Individual	£20
Weekly Charter	£800 (minimum)
Tackle Hire	£5 daily

NOTABLE CAPTURES

Species	Weight (lbs)	Location	Bait	Boat/Shore	Date
Conger	42	Fethard	Mackerel	S	8/86
Rockling	2 lbs 5.72 oz	Rosslare	Mackerel	S	10/86
Cuckoo Wrasse	1 lb 12½ oz	Carne	Ragworm	B	9/88
Cuckoo Wrasse	1.55	Tuskar Rock	Baited feathers	B	5/87
Ballan Wrasse	6 lbs 5.5 oz	Kilmore Quay	Lure	B	9/90
Ballan Wrasse	5.84	Saltees	Ragworm	B	8/86
Flounder	4 lbs 6.5 oz	Ballyteigue	Crab	S	8/79
Flounder	4.01	Cullenstown	Crab	S	11/91
Smouth Hound	7.07	Rosslare Strand	Crab	S	8/91
Bass	11.35	Ballyteigue	Crab	S	6/88
Bass	11	Ferrycarrig	Crab	S	7/88
Pouting	3.40	Kilmore Quay	Baited feathers	B	10/87
Painted Ray	10.98	Rosslare	Mackerel	B	9/87
Scad	1.55	Carnsore	Feathers	B	8/88
Tope	45	Kilmore Quay	Mackerel	B	9/90

IRISH RECORDS

Species	Weight (lbs)	Location	Bait	Boat/Shore	Date
Flounder	4.60	Ballyteigue	Crab	S	11/91
Pouting	4 lbs 13.5 oz	Kilmore Quay	Baited feathers	B	4/83
Cuckoo Wrasse	1.94 lbs	Carne	Ragworm	B	8/91

COMMON SPECIES

Common Species	Average Size Caught (lbs)
Conger	15
Wrasse	3
Pollack	6
Coalfish	3
Spurdog	7
Ling	6

Common Species	Average Size Caught (lbs)
Tope	25
Dogfish	2
Pouting	2
Rockling	1
Cod	5
Ray	8
Smooth Hound	4

■ TACKLE SHOPS

Peter Goggin, 56 South Main Street, New Ross

Jim Mooney and Co. Ltd., 1 North Street, New Ross

George Bridges, 14 Selskar Street, Wexford

Sports Shop, South Street, New Ross

Redmond and Dillon, Main Street, Fethard

■ CLUBS AND CONTACTS

Kilmore SAC, W. McLoughlin, Spencerstown, Clearistown, Co. Wexford, (053) 39168

New Ross SAC, J. Ryan, Ballybrazil, New Ross, Co. Wexford, (051) 21956

Saltee SAC, M. Murphy, 24 Pinewood Estate, Wexford, (053) 41372

Wexford and District SAC, S. Furlong, 117 The Faythe, Wexford

Wexford Garda SAC, J. Coady, Tritonville, Park, Wexford, (053) 43479

Wexford SAC, Mary O'Connor, Ballyvaloo, Blackwater, Co. Wexford

■ COMPETITIONS

This area contains a number of popular shore competition fishing venues. Pegged matches are staged regularly on the Burrow, while the rocks at Hook Head have permanent peg numbers painted on them. Boat competitions are increasing in popularity, and further details can be obtained from club secretaries.

Dunmore East to Youghal

INTRODUCTION

Waterford is a beautiful county and, for many people, it has the added attraction of being off the main tourist circuit. There are mountain ranges in the centre from which short rivers drain down to a coastline which is, typically, high cliffs interrupted by numbers of small coves and three major estuaries. If you want a change from sea angling, the short rivers on the south side of the mountains provide a little seasonal fishing for Sea Trout and Grilse (known locally as Peel). There are some reservoirs and lakes stocked with Trout on which day tickets are available and the River Suir and its tributaries on the north side of the mountains have some important fishing for Salmon and good Wild Brown Trout. The Blackwater, which is the western county boundary, is an important Salmon river and also has fishing for Brown and White Trout in its tributaries. There are a few lakes in the county which hold Pike and Rudd. Belle Lake between Waterford City and Dunmore East is one of the best known, but most of the coarse fishing interest is in the Blackwater in west Waterford, with excellent Roach and Dace.

There is plenty of bed and breakfast accommodation and some hotels and camp sites. But the lack of tourist and angling development means that this accommodation is not always available precisely where the angler wants to be and a car is very useful to the visitor.

To get back to the sea angling, there are three main centres, each coinciding with one of the three major estuaries which have broken gaps in the ramparts of cliff. Starting in the east, the massive estuary of the 'three sisters', the Barrow, the Suir and the Nore, has a major commercial fishing and angling centre at its mouth – the harbour of Dunmore East. This part of the county has charter boats, tackle shops and angling clubs as well as plenty of accommodation.

Heading west, there is a long stretch of beautiful and relatively undeveloped shoreline with a few long strands at places like Tramore and Clonea but a lot of cliffs, small coves and little tidal harbours with boat slips. This is a coastline which is well worth exploring by the enterprising shore angler or a dinghy owner who is experienced and understands the dangers of an exposed Atlantic coast. I have family connections with this part of the country and have spent many happy summer holidays catching Bass and Ray in the little sandy coves, Pollack from the rocky headlands and Mackerel from my dinghy.

At Dungarvan, a much smaller estuary where the River Colligan meets the sea has created a safe harbour out of which charter boats operate, including the most easterly Blue Shark fishery in Ireland. There is also famous Flounder fishing in the estuary and some Bass locally. Helvick Head, to the west of Dungarvan, seems to deflect the North Atlantic Drift offshore and species like Blue Shark follow it.

The stretch of coast between Helvick and Ardmore, because of its inaccessibility, is frankly one of the least interesting stretches of coast for sea anglers in the country. But once you get to Ardmore things change quite dramatically. After all, this is where in April 1977 an English angler took our rod-caught record Bass – 17 lbs 1¼ oz – from the shores of Whiting Bay!

There are also charter boat operators and dinghy launching facilities in Youghal.

Waterford's Bass populations tend to be a little thin on the ground, but the average size of the fish is generally very good. I've taken a fish over the 10 lb specimen weight from the beach at Bunmahon myself, and many smaller ones. Of course, this was before the inshore commercial fishermen thinned them out. But if you meet a small sandy cove with a freshwater stream flowing out, a good surf and night coming on, you could be in for a memorable shore angling experience.

The major centres like Waterford City, Tramore, Dungarvan and Youghal (which is technically just over the county boundary in Cork) have thriving angling clubs these days and their members usually have up-to-the-minute information.

County Waterford has given me some of my most enduring sea angling memories. My biggest ever Bass, 250 lbs of Pollack in one day to a Redgill trolled behind a dinghy, double figure Thornbacks on very light tackle. May it be as kind to you.

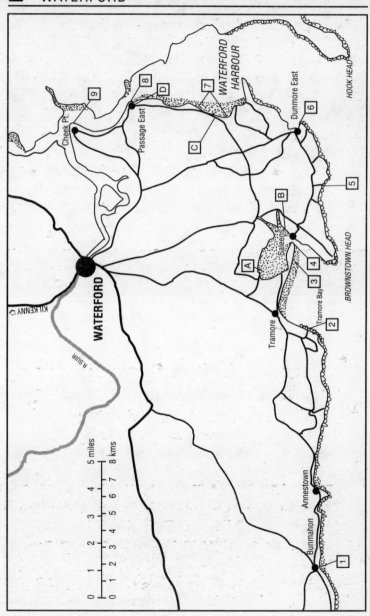

Dunmore East is situated on the south-west side of the lower reaches of Waterford Harbour. It is a large commercial fishing port and also caters for all types of boating activities. The angling here is for mixed fishing, extending to species such as Ray, Pollack, Ling, Conger, Coalfish.

Shore fishing is popular in Waterford harbour, Dunmore East and Tramore. The estuary flowing into the back strand at Tramore has produced a number of specimen Flounder and Bass in recent years. There are many coves and inlets in this area which have produced fish in the past. Generally, however, angling pressure is light.

Waterford Harbour is potentially an excellent small boat angling venue. It is a vast area of comparatively sheltered water which is known to produce Ray, Flatfish, Codling. As yet, the inshore fishing has not been fully explored.

Boat fishing is from April until October and shore fishing is from April until January.

SHORE ANGLING MARKS (map – page 67)

1. BUNMAHON: Bottom fishing for Bass, Flounder, Plaice, Dogfish and occasional Ray. Specimen Thornback Ray and Flounder have been recorded from the beach.
2. WESTTOWN ROCKS: Spinning for Mackerel and Pollack and float fishing for Wrasse. Fishing prohibited at bathing place.
3. TRAMORE STRAND: Surf fishing for Bass and Flatfish at all stages of the tide. Best at high and low water.
4. SALEENS: Bottom fishing for Bass and Flounder below car park. Many specimen Flounder and Bass taken here from this stretch. Fishing all stages of the tide. Mullet in channel.
5. RATHMOYLAND COVE: Bottom fishing for Flounder and Dogfish. Spinning for Pollack on eastern point, especially at high water.

6. DUNMORE EAST: Bottom fishing from either pier for Flounder and Rockling. Specimen Flounder and Rockling recorded here. Night fishing for Conger and float fishing for Mullet using fish bait. Spinning for Pollack and Mackerel from rocks below car park and float fishing for occasional large Wrasse.

7. WOODSTOWN STRAND: Beach fishing for Flatfish, freshwater Eels and some Bass. Specimen Black Sole recorded here. Two hours either side of high water best.

8. PASSAGE EAST: Bottom fishing for Bass and Flatfish at high water. Spinning from bank south of pier for Bass at low water and first two hours of the flood.

9. CHEEKPOINT: Bottom fishing for Flounder and Dogfish. Good fishing for Codling and Coalfish during the winter months.

■ BAIT (map – page 67)

A. TRAMORE BACK STRAND: Lugworm plentiful near dyke wall on north-east tip of back strand. Peeler crab can be collected under weed and stone at outlet from marsh.

B. SALEENS: Soft and peeler crab plentiful under clumps of seaweed on beach north of car park.

C. WOODSTOWN STRAND: Lugworm and some shellfish on beach. Beach strips for over ½ mile.

D. PASSAGE EAST: Ragworm can be dug on mussel banks south of pier.

■ APPROVED BOATS FOR HIRE

There are several part-time boats available in Dunmore East at weekends and possibly at other periods. Anglers will have to make their own arrangements. Contact could be made by ringing Dunmore East SAC, Secretary Joseph Dunphy, (051) 55025.

NOTABLE CAPTURES

Species	Weight (lbs)	Location	Bait	Boat/Shore	Date
Rockling	2.51	Dunmore East	Mackerel	S	8/90
Twaite Shad	2 lbs 5 oz	St Mullin's	Spinner/lure	S	4/90
G Mullet	6.36	Dunmore East	Mackerel	S	8/91
Ballan Wrasse	4.85	Tramore	Ragworm	S	9/90
Bass	10.0	Saleens	Sandeel	S	10/89
Rockling	2.0	Brownstown	Mackerel	S	8/91
Flounder	3.07	Saleens	Lugworm	S	12/89
Garfish	3.32	Dunmore East	Mackerel	S	7/89

IRISH RECORDS

Species	Weight (lbs)	Location	Bait	Boat/Shore	Date
Dab	2.02	Dunmore East	Lugworm	S	1/90
Twaite Shad	2.87	St Mullin's	Lure	S	5/85

COMMON SPECIES

Common Species	Average Size Caught (lbs)
Ling	10
Pollack	7
Coalfish	3
Ray	8
Whiting	1.5
Conger	12
Dogfish	2.5
Flounder	2
Rockling	1
Wrasse	3

■ TACKLE SHOPS

Morgan and Carroll, Waterford City

■ CLUBS AND CONTACTS

Dunmore East SAC, Joseph Dunphy, 68 Grange Heights, Waterford, (051) 55025

Tramore SAC, Tony Power, 286 St John's Park, Waterford, (051) 77899

Waterford Glass SAC, John O'Brien, 5 Orchard Drive, Ursuline Court, Waterford.

Rinnashark SAC, Liam Ryan, 153 Hennessy's Road, Waterford

■ COMPETITIONS

There are many shore and boat competitions throughout the season. Boat competitions are normally held from Dunmore East. For further details, contact club secretaries.

■ DESCRIPTION: DUNGARVAN

Dungarvan Bay faces due east and the town is tucked into the northwestern corner on the banks of the Colligan River. Deep sea angling boats have been operating from the town for a number of years and good fishing has been recorded. Shark, general ground and wreck fishing are all available.

Small boat fishing is increasing in popularity and the main species on offer are Bass, Flatfish, Ray and Dogfish. Shore angling is also very popular and specimen fish have been recorded near the town in recent years.

Wreck fishing, which has been producing excellent results, is on offer all year. General angling is from April until October, with shore fishing extending right up to January.

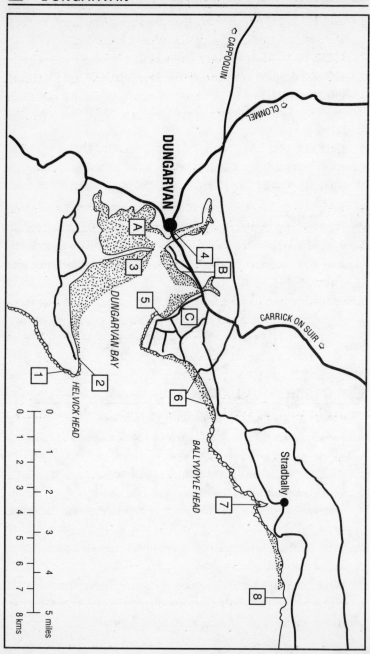

■ SHORE ANGLING MARKS (map – page 72)

1. HELVICK HEAD: Fishing from rocks for Mackerel, Pollack, Wrasse and Conger. Specimen Wrasse recorded.
2. HELVICK PIER: Conger from both pier walls. Mullet on seaward side of pier from late ebb to early flood. Occasional Bass and Flatfish while bottom fishing. Distance casting produces Ray and Dogfish. Specimen Mullet recorded.
3. CUNNIGAR SPIT: Bottom fishing for Bass and Flatfish. Late flood to high water. Spinning for Bass at extreme point of Cunnigar, late flood to high water.
4. RAILWAY BRIDGE: Spinning for Bass and bottom fishing for Flounder above bridge. Specimen Flounder recorded.
5. BALLINACOURTY PIER: Bass, Flatfish and Dogfish from half flood to early ebb. Spinning from reefs behind golf course.
6. CLONEA STRAND: Surf fishing for Bass and Flatfish from low water to early ebb. Spinning from reefs in rocky coves.
7. STRADBALLY: Beach fishing for Bass, Flatfish and Dogfish. Early flood tide best, with moderate surf conditions
8. BALLYDWAN: Beach fishing for Flatfish, Bass, Dogfish and occasional Ray. Rocky patches interspersed on beach.

■ BAIT (map – page 72)

A. DUNGARVAN SWIMMING POOL: Soft and peeler crab plentiful under weed on strand. Some lug can also be dug here.
B. ABBEYSIDE: Crab plentiful under weed south of abbey. Lug in sandy patches.
C. BALLINACOURTY: Lugworm can be dug north of pier. Soft and peeler crab can be collected under weed near rocky reefs.

APPROVED BOATS FOR HIRE

Boat Name	Kingfisher	Sea of Galilea
Skipper/Owner	Cormac Walsh Gone Fishin' Tackle Shop Lower Main Street, Dungarvan	Paddy Riordan Dungarvan Charter Angling Kilossera, Dungarvan
Base	Dungarvan	Dungarvan
Telephone	(058) 43514	(058) 43286
Length	11 m (36 ft)	10.31 m (34 ft)
No. of Anglers	Shark–6 Ground/wreck–8	Shark–6 Ground/wreck–8-10
Facilities	Radio, Radar, Echo Sounder, Navigator, 12 Man Liferaft, Toilet.	Sounder, Radio, Radar, Navigator, Life Jackets, Toilet
Daily Charter	£120 (8 persons) minimum charge £75	£100 minimum charge £75
Daily Individual	£15	£15
Weekly Charter	£800 (7 days)	£600
Tackle Hire	Shark and bottom outfits – £5 daily, £35 weekly	Bottom outfits £5 daily, £20 weekly. Shark outfit £7 daily

There are several other boats available for charter in Dungarvan.

NOTABLE CAPTURES

Species	Weight (lbs)	Location	Bait	Boat/Shore	Date
Flounder	3.40	Dungarvan	Crab	S	12/90
Rockling	1.87	Dungarvan	Mackerel	B	9/90
Ling	27.0	Dungarvan	Mackerel	B	7/89
Flounder	3 lbs 3½ oz	Dungarvan	Lugworm	S	1/89
Bass	13 lbs 1 oz	Helvick	Shrimp	S	8/87
Whiting	3 lbs 1½ oz	Dungarvan	Ragworm	B	8/86
Pouting	3.0	Dungarvan	Mackerel	B	8/86
Plaice	4.2	Dungarvan	Mackerel	B	9/85
Blue Shark	115.0	Dungarvan	Mackerel	B	8/85

COMMON SPECIES

Common Species	Average Size Caught (lbs)
Blue Shark	45
Ling	10
Conger	15
Cod	5
Pouting	1¼
Coalfish	4
Pollack	7
Ray	8
Whiting	1½
Dogfish	2
Garfish	1¼
Flounder	2

TACKLE SHOPS

Gone Fishin' Tackle Shop, Cormac Walsh, Lower Main Street, Dungarvan, (058) 43514

Baumann's Tackle Shop, Sev Baumann, Mary's Street, Dungarvan, (058) 41395

CLUBS AND CONTACTS

Dungarvan SAC, Secretary Damien Dillon, Mitchell Street, Dungarvan, (058) 42806

Abbeyside SAC, Secretary Michael Cowming, 3 Byrneville, Dungarvan, (058) 41011 (work)

Ardmore SAC, Secretary Gerard Mansfield, Green Shutters, Ardmore, (024) 94137

CONTACTS

Cormac Walsh, Gone Fishin' Tackle Shop, Lower Main Street, Dungarvan, (058) 43514

Sev Baumann, Baumann's Tackle Shop, Mary's Street, Dungarvan, (058) 41395

■ COMPETITIONS

There are many boat and shore competitions throughout the season. Many of the boat competitions are open to visitors from July to September. For further details contact the club secretary.

■ DESCRIPTION: YOUGHAL AND ARDMORE

Youghal is situated on the west side of the Blackwater Estuary and is the most easterly town in Co. Cork. It offers deep sea, inshore and shore fishing and is a very popular resort for anglers.

The deep water mark off Capel Island is one of the best areas for Cod on the south coast. Many fine specimen Ling to 38 lbs have been recorded on the offshore wrecks.

The beaches at Ardmore fish particularly well, especially Ballyquinn, for Ray, Flatfish and some Bass. Many specimens have been caught here. The Irish record Bass was caught by British angler Malcolm Tucker at Whiting Bay. Boat fishing is from April until October, with shore fishing extending until January.

■ SHORE ANGLING MARKS (map – page 77)

1. KNOCKADOON HEAD: Spinning and float fishing for Pollack, Mackerel, Wrasse and Mullet. Bottom fishing for Three-bearded Rockling. There is a track down to this mark.

2. PILLMORE: Surf fishing on beach at mouth of estuary for Bass and Flounder. Spinning in main channel for Bass and Sea Trout, bottom fishing for Flounder. Plaice and Codling during winter months from main beach.

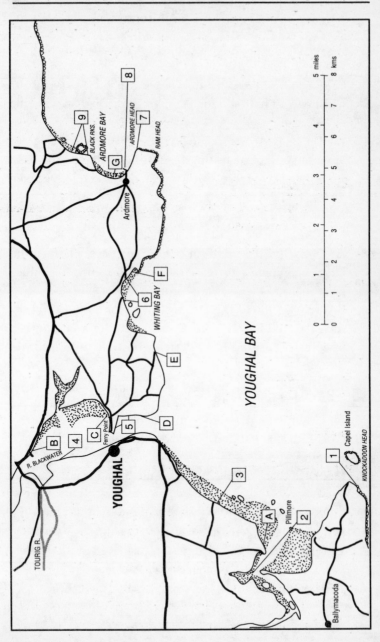

3. YOUGHAL STRAND: Surf fishing for Bass and Flatfish. Codling and Coalfish in winter.

4. OLD DYKE WALL: Very good Flounder fishing from half flood to half ebb. Bottom fishing for Plaice and Cod. Crab bait best.

5. FERRY POINT: Steep shingle beach which fishes well from half flood to half ebb for Flatfish, Bass, Dogfish, Codling and Conger.

6. WHITING BAY: Surf fishing for Bass, Flatfish and Dogfish. Spinning and float fishing from rocky outcrops for Bass, Cod, Pollack, Wrasse, Sea Trout and Mackerel. Specimen Plaice and Bass recorded.

7. ARDMORE HEAD: Spinning and floatfishing for Pollack, Mackerel, Wrasse, Sea Trout and occasional Garfish.

8. ARDMORE PIER: Bottom fishing for Bass, Flatfish and Dogfish. Spinning for Sea Trout and floatfishing for Mullet. Back Sole and Plaice also recorded.

9. BALLYQUINN STRAND: Surf fishing for Bass, Thornback Ray, Painted Ray, Plaice, Dabs, Flounder and Dogfish. Specimen Painted Ray, Plaice, Dogfish and Flounder recorded.

■ BAIT (map – page 77)

A. PILLMORE: Lugworm plentiful below car park.

B. OLD BRIDGE: Good peeler and soft crab in weed covered margins.

C. INSIDE FERRY POINT: Lugworms below tracks (mainly small).

D. MONATRAE: Crab along rocks below Monatrae House.

E. MANGAN'S COVE: Crab can be collected under weed.

F. WHITING BAY: Good lugworm (600 yards to left of car park). Crab can also be collected here.

G. ARDMORE STRAND: Lugworm can be dug on beach.

■ APPROVED BOATS FOR HIRE

Boat Name	Niamh Coran	Paloma
Skipper/Owner	Bernard O'Keefe	Thomas Curtin
	126 North Main Street, Youghal, Co. Cork	Harbour View, Youghal, Co. Cork
Base	Youghal, Co. Cork	Youghal, Co. Cork
Telephone	(024) 92820	(024) 92144 (H) (021) 631208/631793 (W)
Length	8.6 m (28 ft)	9.4 m (31 ft)
No. of Anglers	Shark–6; Bottom–8	Shark–6; Ground–8
Facilities	Echo sounder, Radio, Radar, Navigator, Liferaft, Toilet	Radio, Echo Sounder, Navigator, Life jackets, Flare pack, Toilets, Cooking equipment
Daily Charter	£80 Minimum charge £60	£120 Minimum charge £60
Daily Individual	By arrangement	£15
Weekly Charter	By arrangement	£300
Tackle Hire	Shark £4.00 daily. Bottom tackle £3 daily	Shark and bottom outfits £5.00 daily; £30 weekly

■ NOTABLE CAPTURES

Species	Weight (lbs)	Location	Bait	Boat/Shore	Date
Flounder	3 lbs 1 oz	Youghal	Lugworm	S	9/90
Flounder	3.03	Youghal	Crab	S	10/89
Flounder	3.14	Youghal	Crab	S	10/89
Conger	45.0	Youghal	Mackerel	B	8/89
Cuckoo Wrasse	1.26	Youghal	Baited Feathers	B	8/88
Plaice	7 lbs 1¼ oz	Ardmore	Crab	S	5/87
Homelyn Ray	5.09	Whiting Bay	Mackerel	B	5/87
Blue Shark	66.7 kg	Youghal	Mackerel	B	8/87
Coalfish	16.5	Youghal	Mackerel	B	6/87
Ling	12.9 kg	Youghal	Mackerel	B	10/87
Flounder	3.2	Youghal	Crab	S	4/91

■ IRISH RECORD

Bass	17 lbs 1¼ oz	Whiting Bay	Lugworm	S	4/77

■ COMMON SPECIES

Common Species	Average Size Caught (lbs)
Blue Shark	45
Cod	5
Ling	6
Pollack	5
Coalfish	3
Whiting	1¼
Conger	13
Gurnard	1
Dogfish	2

■ TACKLE SHOPS

Pratt's Arcade Stores, South Main Street, Youghal
Troy's, South Main Street, Youghal

■ CLUBS AND CONTACTS

Ardmore SAC, Mary Moloney, Fountain House, Ardmore, (024) 94188
Youghal SAC, T. Keniry, Ballyhubbard, Youghal, (024) 92210
For small boat fishing, contact Michael Drake, Pope John Place, Youghal.

■ COMPETITIONS

Two main features on the competition calendar are the festival week in July and the Shark Safari in August. For further details, contact T. Keniry.

Ballycotton
& Cork Harbour

Ballycotton is one of those magical names in Irish sea angling. And it's a name with a great pedigree. Back in Edwardian times, when sport angling in salt water was very young, a club called the Dreadnoughts was formed in London. Their aim was to search the wild Atlantic fringes of these islands for monstrous fish to capture on rod and line... and Ballycotton was the base from which they had much of their success. In particular they pioneered the capture of huge Skate on rod and line.

There is still a lot of foreign interest in the boat angling out of the harbour today. But, by another peculiar twist of history, sixty per cent of the foreign anglers who visit Ballycotton today come from the totally land-locked country of Austria. It all has to do with an Austrian national who set up a very successful charter boat business in the quiet East Cork fishing harbour.

Ballycotton has other claims to fame. It holds no less than seven Irish records... and I don't think any other centre can beat that. There is still marvellous boat fishing for Pollack (up to eighteen pounds in recent years) and Conger... though the big Skate have become scarcer. And it also offers some very serious shore fishing. For me, the Mullet in the harbour are a constant distraction because I'm totally addicted to them as a species. They occur in most Irish fishing ports and there is natural groundbaiting from all the fish waste dumped by trawlers and lobster boats. In a situation like this, they're not as difficult to catch as you might think from their reputation... provided you use the right tackle and small scraps of fish or bread soaked in fish oil as a bait.

But to get back to those seven records. The really remarkable thing about them is that three of them are from the shore – and all by one angler! The species are Black Sole, Plaice and Painted Ray, and the angler is, of course, the famous Eddie Cull. Eddie lives in Midleton and is a dedicated and highly imaginative sea angler who hates boats. Despite this, he has six Irish record medals on his mantel-piece; he holds four records and has beaten his own record twice. A shore angler who so consistently beats the boats is a rare thing indeed.

Cork Harbour is a very different kettle of fish. It is a huge expanse of sheltered water, full of commercial shipping and industry. To give you an idea of its size, you can stand at the mouth and look over at the other side, which is about a two mile swim – or a seventy mile drive!

There is great back-up for anglers in the area, with several good charter boats, a complete choice of accommodation, good tackle shops and active clubs.

It must be said that the pressure of commercial fishing and industrial activity in recent years has reduced the quality of the angling on the easier-to-reach marks in the inner harbour. The charter boat operators have reacted to this by equipping themselves with faster craft with sophisticated electronic gear and specialising in wreck fishing. Harbours with this amount of shipping have a corresponding density of wrecks and there is probably no better place in Ireland to base yourself for wrecking. The trouble is that fishing the more exposed marks of the outer harbour, with the pinpoint accuracy needed for wrecking, is rather weather dependent.

The all-round angler will have an answer to weather problems – and there is some quite good game and coarse angling in the East Cork area. The pinnacle of it is probably The Lough in Cork City. The Lough is an extraordinary venue, a pond in a city park which holds the Irish Carp record and produces specimens every year. Fairly specialised but very interesting. There is some other coarse fishing in the River Lee, as well as Salmon, Brown Trout and some Sea Trout. A number of put-and-take rainbow and brown lakes in the area have become popular in recent years. Loughaderry is probably the best known.

All in all, East Cork offers plenty to interest anglers, with the emphasis on the quality charter boat fishing.

◼ DESCRIPTION: BALLYCOTTON

Ballycotton is a picturesque fishing village only forty minutes' drive from Cork. The bay which stretches seven miles between Knockadoon Head and Ballycotton Island is an angler's paradise, with high quality boat and shore fishing available.

Travelling time for boat anglers from the harbour to the fishing grounds is under an hour. Blue Shark, Ray, Ling, Conger, Pollack, Coalfish, Cod, Turbot and occasional Porbeagle and Common Skate are all available. Seven Irish records are held here, three of these from the shore. The boat angling season is normally from May to October, while shore fishing extends from April to January.

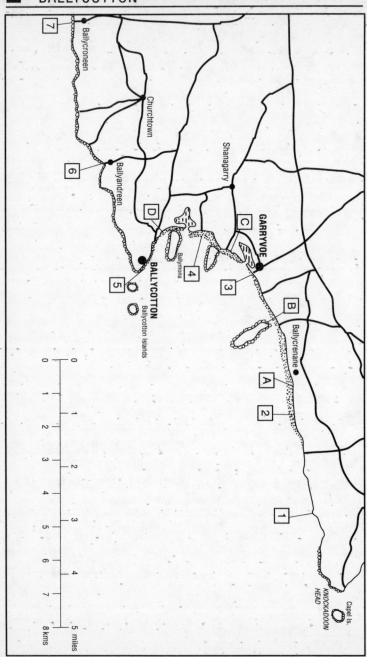

■ SHORE ANGLING MARKS (map – page 84)

1. **BALLYNAKEAGH:** Good spots on the east side of this mark for Wrasse, Dogfish, Rockling and Bass from May to November. Codling and Coalfish in late autumn. Casting onto sandy patches.

2. **BALLYCRENANE:** Surf and bottom fishing for Bass, Flounder, Dabs, Plaice, Ray, Codling and Coalfish.

3. **GARRYVOE:** Bottom fishing in front of caravan park on west and east side of rocks for Bass, Dogfish, Ray and Conger. In front of hotel for Bass, Dogfish, Ray and Conger. Specimen Bass, Flounder and Dogfish recorded here.

4. **BALLYMONA/SILVER STRAND:** Surf fishing for Bass, Flounder and Codling. Two hours either side of high water best. Occasional Conger on Silver Strand. Specimen Flounder recorded here.

5. **BALLYCOTTON:** Conger fishing off main pier, night best. Bottom fishing from breakwater for Plaice, Dabs, Black Sole and Dogfish. Codling in winter. Mullet inside breakwater. Specimen Plaice, Dabs and Black Sole recorded here.

6. **BALLYANDREEN:** Spinning and float fishing for Pollack, Mackerel and Wrasse. Bottom fishing on right hand side onto sand for Flounder, Bass, Codling, and Coalfish.

7. **BALLYCRONEEN:** Various stations for Wrasse, Pollack, Mackerel and occasional Bass float fishing and spinning. Specimen Bass and Dogfish recorded here.

■ BAIT (map – page 84)

A. **BALLYCRENANE:** Lugworm plentiful and easy to dig. Sandeel also in season.

B. **BALLINWILLING:** Peeler and soft crab in rocks to left of car park.

C. **ARDNAHINCH:** Lugworm on beach.

D. **BALLYCOTTON:** Crab in weed margins below old schoolhouse.

■ APPROVED BOATS FOR HIRE

Boat Name	Bavaria	Enbar	Porbeagle
Skipper/Owner	P. Manning, Ballycotton Angling Centre	D. Scharf, Ballycotton Angling Centre	H. O'Donovan, Ballycotton Angling Centre
Base	Ballycotton	Ballycotton	Ballycotton
Telephone	(021) 646773	(021) 646056	(021) 646773
Length	8.3m (27 ft)	6.3 m (21 ft)	7 m (23 ft)
No. of Anglers	Shark–4 Ground/wreck–5	Shark–4 Ground/wreck–5	Shark–4 Ground–5
Facilities	Decca Navigator, VHF Radio, 2 Echo Sounders, Toilet	Echo Sounder, Radio	Echo Sounder, Radio
Daily Charter	£75	£70	£70
Daily Individual	By arrangement	By arrangement	By arrangement
Weekly Charter	By arrangement	By arrangement	By arrangement
Tackle Hire	£3.00 – Bottom Tackle; 5–Shark Tackle Daily	£3–daily Bottom Tackle; £5–Shark	£3.00 daily– Bottom Tackle; £5–Shark

Other boats are also available at weekends and for competitions.

■ NOTABLE CAPTURES

Species	Weight (lbs)	Location	Bait	Boat/Shore	Date
Bass	12.75	Ballycroneen	Toby	S	9/90
Blue Shark	120.00	Ballycotton	Mackerel	B	9/90
Blue Shark	115.00	Ballycotton	Mackerel	B	8/90
Black Sole	2.92	Ballycotton	Cocktail	S	10/89
Cod	27.00	Ballycotton	Mackerel/feathers	B	6/89
Conger	44.00	Ballycotton	Mackerel Fillet	B	7/89
Ling	26.00	Ballycotton	Mackerel	B	7/89
Plaice	4.97	Ballycotton	Cocktail	S	9/89
Blue Shark	105.00	Ballycotton	Mackerel	B	8/91
Blue Shark	150.00	Ballycotton	Mackerel	B	8/88
Blue Shark	103.00	Ballycotton	Mackerel	B	7/91

◼ NOTABLE CAPTURES

Species	Weights (lbs)	Location	Bait	Boat/Shore	Date
Black Sole	6.32	Ballycotton Pier	Prawn	S	12/86
Cod	42	Ballycotton	Feather	B	1921
Mackerel	4 lbs 2 oz	Ballycotton	Mackerel	B	9/79
Plaice	8.23	Ballycotton Pier	Squid	S	1/82
Pollack	19 lbs 3 oz	Ballycotton	Mackerel	B	1904
Painted Ray	14.37	Garryvoe	Mackerel	S	6/80
Common Skate	221	Ballycotton	Mackerel	B	1913

◼ COMMON SPECIES

Common Species	Average Size Caught (lbs)
Blue Shark	45
Conger	18
Pollack	8
Ling	12
Coalfish	3
Cod	6
Whiting	1.5
Dogfish	2
Gurnard	1.5
Garfish	1.5

◼ TACKLE SHOPS

T.H. Sports, Main Street, Midleton
Days, Green Street, Cork
The Tackle Shop, Lavitt's Quay, Cork
Lee Fishing Tackle, Popes Quay, Cork

◼ CLUBS AND CONTACTS

Ballycotton SAC, Sheila Egan, Main Street, Ballycotton
(021) 646786
Aghada SAC (Shore), Eddie Cull, Woodlands, Garryduff,
Midleton, Co. Cork, (021) 631376

Boat contact, Peter Manning, The Angling Centre, Ballycotton, (021) 646773

■ COMPETITIONS

Many boats and shore competitions are held each season in Ballycotton and Garryvoe. For further details contact club secretaries.

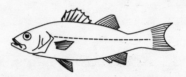

■ DESCRIPTION: CORK HARBOUR

There is a good range of species available in the Cork area. Outside the bay there are Blue Shark, Ling, Cod, Conger, Pollack, Coalfish, Ray, Plaice, Dabs, Pouting, Whiting, Garfish and all the Dogfish.

In the sheltered waters of the harbour the species most frequently taken are Turbot, Ray (especially Blonde Ray), Conger, Plaice, Dabs, Codling and Dogfish. Cork Harbour holds four Irish records: Blonde Ray 36.5 lbs (16.5 kg), Turbot 34 lbs (15 kg), Homelyn Ray 8.28 lbs (3.8 kg) and Dab of 2 lbs (.9 kg).

Wreck fishing is fast developing from all ports within the harbour and many good hauls of fish have been made recently. The wrecks off Power Head in particular have been very productive.

Shore angling too is developing very quickly and has produced a wide range of specimens in recent years. Bass, Flounder, Plaice, Rockling, Whiting and Dab are just some of the species available.

The Irish record Carp was caught in The Lough, Cork City, weighing 26 lbs 2 oz in 1989.

Boat fishing is from April to October, although wreck fishing can be all the year round, weather permitting. Shore fishing is from April to January.

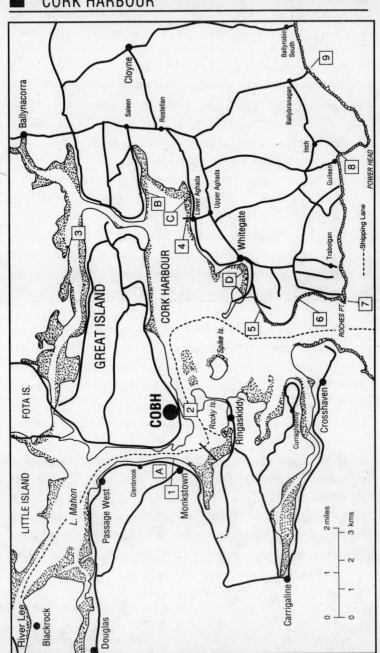

■ CORK HARBOUR

■ SHORE ANGLING MARKS (map – page 89)

1. **SEAWALL, MONKSTOWN:** Bottom fishing for Codling, November to February, bottom fishing for Conger, Ray, Dabs and Dogfish June to September.

2. **DEEPWATER QUAY:** Bottom fishing for Conger, Ray, Codling, Whiting, Dabs, Flounder, Coalfish and Three Bearded Rockling. Best baits crab, fish bait and mussel. Specimen Flounder, Dabs, Whiting and Three Bearded Rockling recorded here.

3. **BROWN'S ISLAND:** Bottom fishing for Thornback Ray, Plaice, Flounder and Dogfish. Crab and fish bait best. Start of flood tide for flatfish most productive.

4. **LOWER AGHADA PIER:** Bottom fishing for Flounder, Dabs and Dogfish. Conger at night. Codling November to February. Float fishing for Mullet.

5. **CARLISLE PIER:** Bottom fishing and spinning for Pollack, Mackerel, Bass, Flatfish and Codling. Thornback and Homelyn Ray also caught here. Crab most efficient bait.

6. **WHITE BAY:** Surf fishing for Bass, Flatfish, Dogfish and occasional Ray. Specimen Plaice recorded from here.

7. **ROCHES POINT:** Spinning for Bass, Pollack and Mackerel. Bottom fishing for Conger and Three Bearded Rockling. Float fishing for Wrasse. Specimen Bass and Wrasse recorded here.

8. **INCH:** Bottom fishing for Bass, Flatfish and Codling. Sandeel available in season. Specimen Bass and Flounder recorded here.

9. **BALLYBRANAGAN:** Bottom fishing for Bass and Flatfish. Turbot to 1½ lb caught at start of flood. Float fishing for Bass from rock first quarter of flood tide. Specimen Bass recorded here.

■ BAIT (map – page 89)

A. **GLENBROOK:** Crab can be collected at low water springs.

B. **SALEEN TO EAST FERRY:** Lugworm. Soft and peeler crab under weed.

C. ROSTELLAN TO LOWER AGHADA PIER: Good lug digging.

D. WHITEGATE BAY: Lugworm plentiful, but small.

■ APPROVED BOATS FOR HIRE

Boat Name	Leaca Rua	Crystal Star
Skipper/Owner	John and Finbarr Barry Cork Harbour Boats, Glenbrook, Passage West, Cork	John & Finbarr Barry Cork Harbour Boats, Glenbrook, Passage West, Cork
Base	Glenbrook	Glenbrook
Telephone	(021) 841348/841633	(021) 841348/841633
Length	11 m (36 ft)	11 m (36 ft)
No. of Anglers	Shark 6–8; Wreck–8 Ground 8–10	Shark 6–8; Wreck–8 Ground/wreck 8–10
Facilities	Sounder, Radar, Radio, Navigator, Liferaft, Toilet	Sounder, Radar, Radio, Navigator, Liferaft, Toilet
Daily Charter	£95–Low season; £100 –High (minimum charge £75)	£95–Low season; £100 –High (minimum charge £75)
Daily Individual	By arrangement	By arrangement
Weekly Charter	£665	£665
Tackle Hire	Shark and bottom – £3 daily; £18 Weekly	Shark and bottom – £3 daily; £18 Weekly

Boat Name	Whispering Hope	Monica T
Skipper/Owner	Barry Twomey, Whispering Pines Guesthouse, Crosshaven	Barry Twomey, Whispering Pines Guesthouse, Crosshaven
Base	Crosshaven	Crosshaven
Telephone	(021) 831448; Fax 831448	(021) 831448; Fax 831448
Length	14.8 m (49 feet)	16 m (52 ft)
No. of Anglers	Shark 6–8 Bottom/Wreck 8–10	Shark 6–8; Bottom/Wreck 8–10
Facilities	Echo sounder, Radar, Radio, Navigator, Life jackets, Toilet	Echo sounder, Radar, Radio, Navigator, Life jackets, Toilet
Daily Charter	£110	£110
Daily Individual	£16	£16
Weekly Charter	By arrangement	By arrangement
Tackle Hire	Shark & Bottom tackle £4	Shark & Bottom tackle £4

Boat Name	Norma T	St Peter
Skipper/Owner	Barry Twomey Whispering Pines Guesthouse, Crosshaven	C. Robinson Boycetown, Carrigaline
Base	Crosshaven	Crosshaven
Telephone	(021) 831448; Fax 831448	(021) 372473/372896
Length	11 m (36 ft)	11 m (36 ft)
No. of Anglers	Shark–6 Ground/Wreck–8	Shark–6 Ground/Wreck–8
Facilities	Radio, Navigator, Radar, Echo Sounder, Toilet, Life jackets	Echo Sounder, Radio, Radar, Navigator, Toilet, Life jackets
Daily Charter	£100	£100
Daily Individual	£16	By arrangement
Weekly Charter	By arrangement	£560– 7 days
Tackle Hire	Shark and Bottom tackle £4	£3 daily

Boat Name	Lagosta II	Three Boys	Trident Star
Skipper/Owner	Brian Byrne Loughcarrig House, Ballinacurra, Midleton,	Patrick J Murphy 8 Riverside Park, Midleton, Courtmacsherry	Michael O'Mahony Kilcrone Midleton, Courtmacsherry
Base	East Ferry	East Ferry	East Ferry
Telephone	(021) 631952	(021) 632594	(021) 631926
Length	10.6 m (35 feet)	10.6 m (35 feet)	13 m (42 feet)
No. of Anglers	Shark–5 Ground/Wreck–8	Shark–6 Bottom–8;Wreck–8	Shark–6-8 Bottom 8-10
Facilities	Echo sounder, Radar, Radio, Navigator, 14–Man Liferaft, Toilet, Cooker etc.	Radio, Echo Sounder, Navigator, Liferaft, Life jackets, Toilet, Washup	Radio, Radar, Navigator, Echo Sounder, Life jackets, Toilet
Daily Charter	£140–Inshore; £200– Offshore wrecks	£90	£100
Daily Individual	£25	£15	£15
Weekly Charter	Above prices x7	£600	
Tackle Hire	£3 daily; Shark and bottom tackle	Shark and bottom tackle - £3 daily; £21 weekly	£3–daily Shark and bottom tackle

Other boats are also available at weekends and for competitions.

■ NOTABLE CAPTURES

Species	Weight (lbs)	Location	Bait	Boat/Shore	Date
Bass	10.73 kg	Inch Bay	Lugworm	S	10/91
Coalfish	17¾	Crosshaven	Baited Feathers	B	8/90
Conger	45.0	East Ferry	Mackerel	B	5/90
Dab	1.55	Crosshaven	Mackerel/Lugworm	S	1/90
Garfish	2 lbs 12½ oz	East Ferry	Mackerel	B	8/90
Ling	41.0	East Ferry	Mackerel	B	7/90
Pollack	14 lbs 1 oz	Crosshaven	Mr Twister	B	7/90
Blue Shark	118.0	Crosshaven	Mackerel	B	7/90
Megrim	1.85	Crosshaven	Mackerel	B	7/89
Rockling	1.98	Crosshaven	Mackerel	B	10/89
Tub Gurnard	5.21	Crosshaven	Mackerel	B	7/89
Plaice	4 lbs 5¼ oz	Cork Harbour	Lugworm	S	11/88
Pollack	12.27	Crosshaven	Mackerel	B	8/91
Cod	35.0	East Ferry	Mackerel	B	6/91
Whiting	3 lbs 7 oz	Crosshaven	Feathers	B	7/88

■ IRISH RECORDS

Species	Weight (lbs)	Location	Bait	Boat/Shore	Date
Blonde Ray	36.5	Cork Harbour	Mackerel	B	9/64
Homelyn Ray	8.28	Cork Harbour	Mackerel	S	9/83
Turbot	34.0	Cork Harbour	Mackerel	B	6/82
Carp	26.2	The Lough, Cork City	Boilie	S	5/89

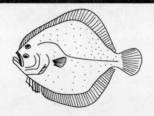

COMMON SPECIES

Common Species	Average Size Caught (lbs)
Blue Shark	45
Pollack	7
Conger	20
Ling	15
Coalfish	6
Garfish	1.5
Turbot	5
Blonde Ray	9
Cod	6
Whiting	1½

TACKLE SHOPS

Murrays, Patrick Street, Cork

Days, Patrick Street, Cork

Walls, Main Street, Whitegate

T.H. Sports, Midleton

Peter Horne, Woodleigh, Killard, Blarney, Cork (021) 85072

The Tackle Shop, Lavitt's Quay, Cork

CLUBS AND CONTACTS

Aghada SAC, Edmund Cull, Woodlands, Garryduff, Midleton, (021) 631376

Cobh SAC, Mary Geary, Sycamore Cottage, Ballynoe, Cobh, (021) 812167

Crosshaven SAC, John Martin, 65 Arbour Heights, Waterpark, Carrigaline, Co. Cork, (021) 371956

Monkstown SAC, Matt Kearney, Beach Road, Passage West, Co. Cork (021) 841190

COMPETITIONS

There are many angling clubs in the Cork Harbour area. Some of the above clubs host international boat and shore competitions throughout the season. For further information on clubs not mentioned, contact Munster Secretary of IFSA John Martin, (021) 371956.

Kinsale & Courtmacsherry

INTRODUCTION

The shoreline between Cork Harbour and Kinsale is rugged. Access for shore angling is difficult and largely not worth the effort. But when Kinsale harbour opens up, you're suddenly in the middle of a major boat angling centre with a most sophisticated infrastructure of restaurants, hotels and guesthouses. This is a tourist town, but very attractive and with plenty to offer non-angling family members.

This is probably the best known centre for Blue Shark fishing around the coast. In fact, the chances of hooking a shark are equally good at any one of half a dozen centres from Dungarvan round to Clare. But Kinsale has the reputation, and some excellent boat operators with a lot of experience of our largest common angling species.

There's a great attraction to sharking. It has to do with the power and reputation of the fish and the fact that they offer a budget-priced introduction to big game fishing without having to travel to tropical waters. Our sharks are also a good size. They average from about forty-five pounds, which means they can be taken on without exotic tackle. But there are a few things that surprised me the first time I tried this type of angling. When I saw my first Blue Shark, what impressed me was not its size or its power or the famous teeth; it was the sheer beauty of the brilliant blue, streamlined shape. I was really glad when it was returned to the sea unharmed.

Blue Shark fishing is normally done on the drift about ten miles out to sea. 'Rubby-dubby' is used to attract the fish. This, of course, is a rather revolting mixture of mashed-up fish bits, fish oil and bran. The smell of the rubby-dubby, combined with the motion of a boat drifting on the long Atlantic swells, makes for a situation where even good sailors are recommended to take one of the very good modern drugs to counteract sea-sickness.

But there is one fringe benefit of the rubby-dubby. It also attracts Garfish, and these gamey little fellows give great sport on fish scraps free-lined on very light tackle while you're waiting for the Blues. It's better to bring your own tackle for the Gars. I once lost what would undoubtedly have been a new Irish record because the six-pound line on the reel had been lying in the sun in the wheelhouse of the boat for years; it parted like a thread as I tried to swing my three foot monster over the gunwale.

But fishing for Blues during the short summer sharking season is by no means all that Kinsale has to offer. The other great attractions are the Ling Rocks, an hour's steaming from the harbour entrance, where British anglers have pioneered light tackle sport for big Pollack, and the wreck of the *Lusitania*, twelve miles south of the Old Head. The *Lusitania* is an 850 foot liner which was torpedoed in the First World War. The wonderful fishing it offers today is undoubtedly under-utilised.

There's also very varied shore fishing in the area. There are good rock marks along the Old Head. The Bandon estuary offers Flounder and what the commercial fishermen have left out of a fine Bass population. There's winter fishing for Codling, Coalies and Flats and a surf beach at Garretstown.

Courtmacsherry, which is the bay on the west side of the Old Head, has similar fishing to Kinsale, with perhaps a little more variety. But it is a place with a totally different atmosphere. While Kinsale is bustling, touristy, sophisticated and cosmopolitan, Courtmacsherry is a sleepy little place with a real West Cork atmosphere which reeks of its main industry – sea angling. Again there are good charter boats and they can operate even in quite brisk sou-westerlies because of the shelter. The Courtmacsherry operators can also add Thornbacks and their big brothers, Common Skate, to the list of fish commonly caught in Kinsale. And the list of shore species is augmented by some really wonderful Mullet fishing downstream of the abattoir at Timoleague Bridge on the Argideen River. A number of specimen Flounders and Bass have come from the beaches round here and in autumn the Flounder fishing can be spectacular.

To top it all off, the all-round angler has game fishing for Salmon, Sea Trout and Brown Trout available in the Bandon River.

So, two major angling centres, both offering excellent fishing and a real choice of atmosphere and character – things which are of real importance in planning an angling holiday.

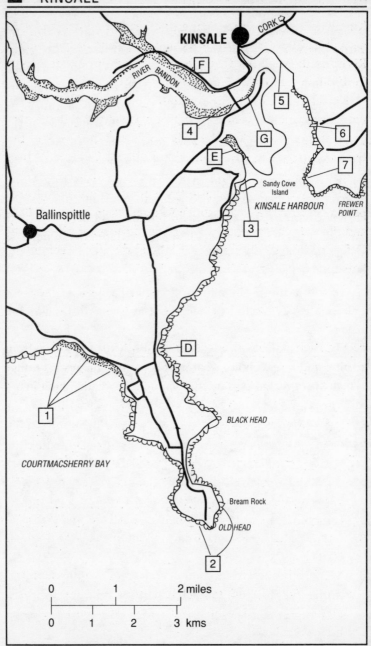

KINSALE

CORK

RIVER BANDON

F

4

5

6

G

E

7

Sandy Cove Island

KINSALE HARBOUR

FREWER POINT

3

Ballinspittle

D

BLACK HEAD

1

COURTMACSHERRY BAY

Bream Rock

OLD HEAD

2

| 0 | | 1 | | 2 miles |

| 0 | 1 | 2 | 3 kms |

■ DESCRIPTION: KINSALE

Kinsale is a picturesque town at the head of a deep and safe natural harbour. The town is located on a bend of the Bandon River estuary which flows between the impressive twin fortifications of Charles Fort and James Fort.

Kinsale has earned the reputation as one of the premier Blue Shark angling centres in Europe. General fishing is also good, and marks such as the Ling Rocks and the wreck of the *Lusitania* produce specimen size Pollack, Coalfish, Ling, Conger etc.

Some good catches have been made from the shore, particularly in the estuary above Kinsale where specimen Bass and Flounder have been recorded. The boat season is April to October, while shore angling can extend through to the end of January.

■ SHORE ANGLING MARKS (map – page 98)

1. GARRETSTOWN: Surf fishing for Bass and Flatfish. The stretch of beach adjacent to Laherne Rock is best. Good surf conditions required. Spinning for Bass and Sea Trout at Corlaun Rock. Specimen Flounder recorded here.
2. OLD HEAD: Rock fishing on western side of lighthouse for Wrasse, Mackerel, Dogfish and occasional Conger. On the southeast side fishing is for Pollack, Coalfish, Mackerel, Wrasse, occasional Dogfish and Conger. Fishing at Gunhole Cove for Pollack, Coalfish, Mackerel and Wrasse.
3. SANDY COVE: Fishing from rock onto sand for Dogfish, Flatfish and Codling.
4. NEW BRIDGE: Fishing into deep water at southern end of bridge for Codling, Pollack, Coalfish, Whiting, Dogfish, Flounder and occasional Bass. Two hours either side of high water best.

5. SALMON WALK: Fishing into main channel for Dogfish, Plaice, Dabs and Flounder. Ray and Conger at night.
6. MIDDLE COVE: Bottom fishing for Dogfish, Bull Huss and occasional Ray and Codling.
7. HARBOUR ENTRANCE: Bottom fishing from point for Dogfish, Wrasse, Dab, Conger, Codling, freshwater Eel, Mackerel, Coalfish and Garfish.

■ BAIT (map – page 98)

D. OLD HEAD PIER: Lugworm on sandy patches near pier and some crab in rocky outcrops.
E. SANDYCOVE: Lugworm and clam can be dug at top of inlet. Some crab under weed on north-east shore.
F. JAGOES POINT: Soft and peeler crab on weedy banks in vicinity of Bridge View house.
G. CASTLEPARK: Crab (soft and peeler) under weed on beach under main road.

■ APPROVED BOATS FOR HIRE

Boat Name	Shamrock Gannet	Mary Rose
Skipper/Owner	Fiona Donaldson Kinsale Marine Services, Lr O'Connell St, Kinsale	Butch Roberts Trident Angling Centre, Trident Hotel, Kinsale
Base	Kinsale	Kinsale
Telephone	(021) 772611 Fax (021) 772611	(021) 774099
Length	11 m (36 ft)	9 m (30 ft)
No. of Anglers	Shark–6 Ground 6–8	Shark–6 Ground 6–8
Facilities	Echo Sounder, Radar, Radio, Toilet, Life jackets	Echo Sounder, Radio, Navigator, Toilet, Life jackets
Daily Charter	£100	£90
Daily Individual	£17; Minimum £60	£18
Weekly Charter	By arrangement	£630
Tackle Hire	£4 daily	£4 daily

Boat Name	Squezi 1	Enterprise
Skipper/Owner	Tom van Heteren Trident Hotel, Kinsale	Reg Bradley Trident Angling Centre, Trident Hotel, Kinsale
Base	Kinsale	Kinsale
Telephone	(021) 774099	(021) 774099
Length	10 m (33 ft)	13 m (42 ft)
No. of Anglers	Shark–6 Ground –8	Shark–6 Ground 8–9
Facilities	Echo Sounder, Radio, Radar, Decca Navigator, Liferaft, Toilet	Sounder, Radar, Radio, Navigator, Toilet, Life jackets
Daily Charter	£100	£120
Daily Individual	£18	£18
Weekly Charter	£700	By arrangement
Tackle Hire	£4 daily	£4 daily

Boat Name	Barracuda	Kern
Skipper/Owner	Pat Collins Kinsale Marine Services, (also Trident Hotel)	Dennis Collins, Kinsale Marine Services, Lr. O'Connell St, Kinsale
Base	Kinsale	Kinsale
Telephone	(021) 772611 Fax (021) 772611	(021) 772611 Fax (021) 772611
Length	10 m (33 ft)	11 m (36 ft)
No. of Anglers	Shark–6 Ground –6	Shark–6 Ground 6-8
Facilities	Sounder, Radio, Radar, Decca Navigator, Toilet, Life jackets	Echo Sounder, Radio, Radar, Toilet, Life jackets
Daily Charter	£100	£100
Daily Individual	£17; Minimum £60	£17; Minimum £6
Weekly Charter	By arrangement	By arrangement
Tackle Hire	£4 daily	£4 daily

NOTABLE CAPTURES

Species	Weight	Location	Bait	Boat/Shore	Date
Ling	11.8 kg	Kinsale	Mackerel	B	7/90
Pollack	5.9 kg	Kinsale	Mackerel Strip	B	8/90
Blue Shark	59.38 kg	Kinsale	Mackerel	B	7/90
Blue Shark	55.7 kg	Kinsale	Mackerel	B	7/90
Ballan Wrasse	5.27 lbs	Old Head	Crab	S	9/90
Ballan Wrasse	5.55 lbs	Old Head	Mackerel	S	8/89
Pollack	12.02 lbs	Kinsale	Spinner	B	9/89
Blue Shark	51.30 kg	Kinsale	Mackerel	B	8/89
Blue Shark	46.35 kg	Kinsale	Mackerel	B	7/89
Garfish	2 lbs 4 oz	Kinsale	Mackerel	B	9/89
Stone Basse	10 lbs 13 oz	Kinsale	Baited Feathers	B	8/89

IRISH RECORDS

Species	Weight	Location	Bait	Boat/Shore	Date
Stone Basse	10 lbs 13 oz	Kinsale	Baited Feathers	B	8/89
Coalfish	12.5 kg	Kinsale	Feathers	B	9/83
Garfish	3 lb 10.25 oz	Kinsale	Lure	B	9/67
Haddock	10 lb 13.5 oz	Kinsale	Mackerel	B	7/64
Ling	46 lb 8oz	Kinsale	Mackerel	B	7/65
Thornback Ray	37 lbs	Ling Rocks	Mackerel	B	5/61
Six Gilled Shark	154 lbs	Kinsale	Mackerel	B	8/68

COMMON SPECIES

Common Species	Average Size Caught (lbs)
Blue Shark	45
Pollack	6
Coalfish	4
Ling	9
Conger	12
Whiting	2
Cod	4
Garfish	1.5
Pouting	1.5
Ray	7
Dogfish	2

TACKLE SHOPS

Kinsale Marine Services, Lr O'Connell Street, Kinsale
(021) 772611

Trident Angling Centre, Trident Hotel, Kinsale, (021) 774099

CLUBS AND CONTACTS

Kinsale SAC, Ingrid van Heteren, Compass Hill, Kinsale,
(021) 774190

Old Head SAC, V. McDwyer, 66 Carrigmore, Carrigaline, Co.
Cork, (021) 372631

COMPETITIONS

Several boat competitions are held in the waters off Kinsale.
For further details, contact the club secretary.

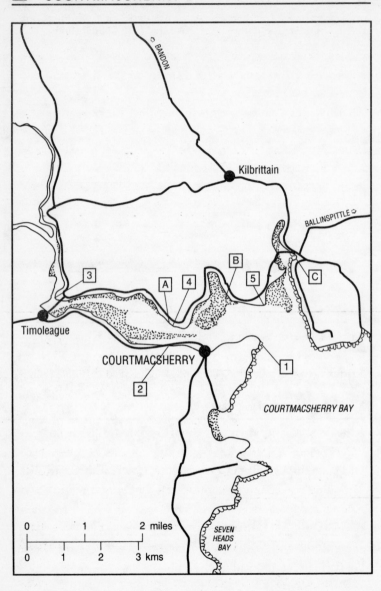

■ DESCRIPTION: COURTMACSHERRY

Courtmacsherry lies to the west side of the Old Head of Kinsale and is on the southern end of the four mile long Argideen Estuary. It is a village resort and is very popular with anglers with virtually all local activities centred around sea angling.

Shark angling is a very popular pursuit with visitors during the summer months. The Seven Heads and the wreck of the *Lusitania* offer good general fishing for specimen sized Pollack, Coalfish, Ling, Conger and Thornback Ray.

Many specimen Bass and Flounder have been recorded by shore anglers in recent years in the estuary. The nearby headlands provide Wrasse, Pollack, Conger and Mackerel during the summer months. The boat season is from April to October, and shore fishing for Flounder and Bass continues up to January.

■ SHORE ANGLING MARKS (map – page 104)

1. WOODPOINT: Spinning for Pollack and Mackerel; bottom fishing for Dogfish.
2. SCHOOL HOUSE: Fishing into channel for Bass and Flounder. Late ebb to early flood best. Specimen Bass and Flounder recorded here.
3. TIMOLEAGUE: Bottom fishing and drifting for Bass in pool below Argideen River Bridge and in channel. Two hours either side of high water best. Floatfishing for Mullet from quay wall and bottom fishing for Flounder. Specimen Bass recorded here.
4. BURREN PIER: Bottom fishing for Bass and Flounder. First three hours of flood best. Specimen Flounder recorded here.
5. HARBOUR VIEW: Spinning and bottom fishing from rocks over sand for Bass and occasional Sea Trout. Bottom fishing for Flounder.

A. BURREN PIER: Some crab around base of pier and on channel banks to west.
B. FLAXFORT STRAND: Lugworm below roadway.
C. KILBRITTAIN: Lugworm on banks of channel.

■ APPROVED BOATS FOR HIRE

Boat Name	Valhalla	Mark Antony	Security
Skipper/Owner	Mark Gannon c/o Woodside Guesthouse, Courtmacsherry	Mark Gannon Woodside Guesthouse, Courtmacsherry	B. O'Donovan, c/o Woodside Guesthouse, Courtmacsherry
Base	The Pier, Courtmacsherry	The Pier, Courtmacsherry	The Pier, Courtmacsherry
Telephone	(023) 46427	(023) 46427	(023) 46427/46363
Length	12 m (39.5 ft)	10 m (33 ft)	9.4 m (31 ft)
No. of Anglers	Shark–6 Ground–8 Wreck–8	Shark–6 Ground–6 Wreck–6	Shark–6 Ground–5 Wreck–6
Facilities	Radio, Echo-Sounder, Liferaft and life jackets, Radar, Navigator, Toilet	Radio, Echo Sounder, Life saving equipment, Toilet, Navigator	Radio, Echo Sounder, Life saving equipment, Toilet
Daily Charter	£100; Wreck fishing – £120 (min. charge £60)	£100; Wreck fishing – £120 (min. charge £60)	£100; Wreck fishing – £120 (min. charge £60)
Daily Individual	£18	£18	£18
Weekly Charter	£700	£700	£700
Tackle Hire	£3 daily; £21 weekly	£3–daily £21 weekly	£3–daily £21 weekly

Other boats are also available at weekends and for competitions.

NOTABLE CAPTURES

Species	Weight (lbs)	Location	Bait	Boat/Shore	Date
Bull Huss	18.0	Courtmacsherry	Mackerel	B	7/90
Flounder	3 lbs 1¾ oz	Argideen Estuary	Crab	S	4/90
Blue Shark	116.0	Courtmacsherry	Mackerel	B	8/90
Blue Shark	110.0	Courtmacsherry	Mackerel	B	8/90
Bass	12 lbs 13 oz	Argideen Estuary	Lugworm	S	12/89
Thornback Ray	22.0	Courtmacsherry	Mackerel	B	6/91
Stone Basse	10.0	Courtmacsherry	Mackerel	B	8/89
Ling	42.0	Courtmacsherry	Mackerel	B	9/91
Ling	30.0	Courtmacsherry	Mackerel	B	10/91
Conger	45.0	Courtmacsherry	Mackerel	B	9/89
Coalfish	19.0	Courtmacsherry	Mackerel	B	6/88

IRISH RECORDS

Electric Ray	69.0	Courtmacsherry	Mackerel	B	9/77
Garfish	1.0	Courtmacsherry	Mackerel	B	7/89
(B. Svetovidovi)					

COMMON SPECIES

Common Species	Average Size Caught (lbs)
Blue Shark	45
Pollack	7
Coalfish	6
Ling	12
Thornback Ray	15
Conger	15
Garfish	1.5
Wrasse	3
Dogfish	2
Whiting	1.5

■ TACKLE SHOPS

Courtmacsherry Sea Angling Centre, The Pier, c/o Mark Gannon, (021) 46427

■ CLUBS AND CONTACTS

Boat angling, Mark Gannon, Woodside, Courtmacsherry (023) 46427
Courtmacsherry SAC, Patricia Gannon, Woodside, Courtmacsherry, (023) 46427
West Cork Sea Anglers SAC, Catherine Lordan, Lakefield House, Castlelack, Bandon (023) 330138

■ COMPETITIONS

Many boat and shore competitions are run by the clubs. One such event worth a mention is the week-long festival, normally held in August. This week caters for serious boat and shore anglers as well as ladies, juveniles, even a crab competition for small children. For further details, contact club secretary Patricia Gannon.

Clonakilty to Mizen Head

INTRODUCTION

This chapter covers the long, untidy coastline of West Cork, right out to the 'big toe' of Ireland at Mizen Head. It's an area of great beauty, relaxed atmosphere and mixed angling. It's a part of the country that has its own definite identity and its friendliness to strangers has attracted many 'blow-ins' – foreigners, some of whom have started by owning holiday homes and ended up living full time in this most southwesterly extremity of the country.

The fishing is mixed, but the back-up in terms of bait, tackle and accommodation is better than might be expected and the resourceful angler need never be short of anything.

Starting in Clonakilty, Ring Harbour has boat fishing from a charter boat and dinghies and some excellent shore fishing off fine beaches for a limited range of species. Specimen Bass and Flounder are the main quarry.

Farther west, the Rosscarbery estuary adds Mullet to this list. The great storm beaches in the area don't hold as many Bass as they used to, but are still worth fishing if you avoid fine summer days when the beaches are covered in trippers.

Lough Hyne is an amazing place, worth a visit if you never fished it. It's a marine national park, but this doesn't prevent angling. And it's the only place I know where you can fish from the shore into what looks like a lake but is actually a saltwater lagoon over thirty fathoms deep. So you can stand on the shore with oak trees over your head and catch deep water species like Ling.

Baltimore has charter boats that venture out as far as the Fastnet and have more sheltered ground in the lee of the offshore islands for days when the Atlantic is less kindly. Recent drainage work on the River Ilen which flows into the sea here doesn't seem to have helped the Salmon and Mullet fishing.

Roaring Water Bay is a spot I'd recommend anglers to avoid. It looks great but I know of three top anglers who fished it stubbornly for a week and caught between them a grand total of six Dogfish – or maybe the same Dogfish six times.

Schull is the capital of the Mizen Peninsula proper and offers some interesting fishing. The boats record a great variety of species. One operator recorded thirty in a recent season. These include unusual Gulf Stream fish like Hake and Red and Black Bream, but the mainstay is superb Pollack and Shark.

The shore fishing is not quite as good but, again, there is great variety. There's rock, beach and pier fishing and plenty of bait for the angler prepared to get it himself. The south side of the peninsula fishes better than the north and, as the area is not the best surveyed in the country, it's always possible to end up on a virgin mark. Ray and Huss are probably the principal shore species, but the Bass angler who likes to explore can do very well along this coast.

Although this is a holiday area, the Mizen is so big and wild that it's always possible to get away from the crowds and fish in solitude, surrounded by the magnificent seascapes. There is a high density of guest houses and self-catering accommodation, but some of them are booked well in advance and others tend to be a bit pricey. If you have any accommodation difficulties,

Bantry, which is covered in the next chapter, is only a short drive away and always seems to have vacancies.

The all-round angler should note that one of the features of West Cork is a lot of small-town reservoirs. Many of these have been stocked with Brown and Rainbow Trout by the Southwestern Regional Fisheries Board.

West Cork is a long way away for most people, but it's such an unusual place, with such idiosyncratic fishing, that anglers in the know tend to think that it's worth the drive.

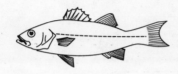

▪ DESCRIPTION: CLONAKILTY

The town of Clonakilty is situated at the head of a large shallow estuary. Six miles to the west is the picturesque inlet of Rosscarbery. Both these areas are very popular with summer visitors. The deep sea fishing produces a wide variety of species, including Blue Shark. There are several wrecks within easy reach and these produce large Conger and Ling.

The two main features for shore anglers are Rosscarbery and Clonakilty estuaries which offer excellent Flounder and Bass fishing. In recent years, both these areas have yielded specimen Flounder and Bass. The third largest Bass taken in Irish waters was recorded at the Bar Rock, Clonakilty. This fish weighed 16 lbs 3 oz and was taken by an English angler in October 1983.

Boat angling is normally from April to October, and shore angling continues right up to the end of January.

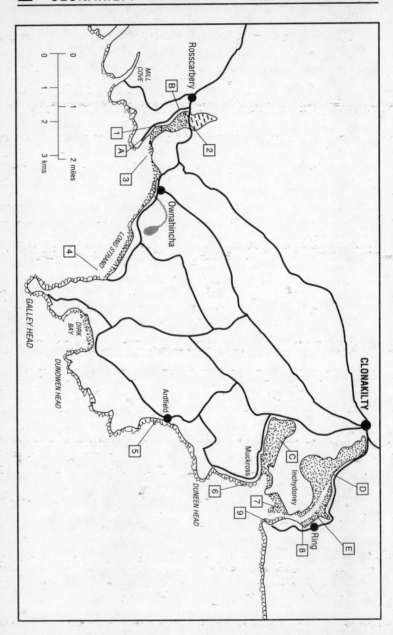

SHORE ANGLING MARKS (map – page 112)

1. ROSSCARBERY: Bottom fishing at boat slip for Flounder. Spinning and bottom fishing for occasional Bass. Early flood to high water best. Float fishing for Mullet at low water in pool above slip and ground baiting is essential. Also bottom fishing off main pier for Flounder, Dogfish and some Bass.

2. ROSSCARBERY (ROAD BRIDGE): Float fishing for Mullet on both sides of bridge. Ground bait with flakes of bread.

3. WARREN STRAND: Bottom fishing for Flounder at channel end on the flood tide. Surf fishing on main part of the beach for Flounder and Bass. Ray and Dogfish taken during summer months, especially at night and flood tide best.

4. THE LONG STRAND (EAST): Surf fishing for Flatfish and occasional Bass, especially at river mouth. Low water and first of ebb best.

5. DUNNYCOVE BAY: Bottom fishing for Flatfish, Dogfish and Bass. Distance casting produces Ray. All stages of the tide.

6. MUCKROSS HEAD: Bottom fishing for Flounder and occasional Bass.

7. CLONAKILTY ESTUARY: Bottom fishing for Bass and Flounder. Last of ebb and first two hours of flood best.

8. RING HARBOUR: Drift lining for Bass, plus bottom fishing for Flounder, at early flood to high water. Specimen Flounder recorded here.

9. BAR ROCK: Spinning and bottom fishing for Bass and Flounder. Last hour of ebb and first two hours of flood best. Bass over 16 lbs have been recorded here.

BAIT (map – page 112)

A. ROSSCARBERY: Sandeel in channel upstream of pier.

B. ROSSCARBERY: Lugworm can be dug on sand and mud flats below road bridge.

C. MUCKROSS ESTUARY: Lugworm can be dug on sandbanks near the road.

113

D. CLONAKILTY ESTUARY: Lugworm can be dug on sandbanks.

E. RING: Crab can be collected under weed between Ring pier and Arundermills.

■ APPROVED BOAT FOR HIRE

Boat Name	Johnboy
Skipper/Owner	Patrick Houlihan, 3–4 Connolly St, Clonakilty, West Cork
Base	Ring (2 miles from Clonakilty)
Telephone	(023) 33654
Length	9.8 (32 ft)
No. of Anglers	Shark–6; Ground–8; Wreck–8
Facilities	Radio, Echo Sounder, Radar, Navigator, Life jackets, Toilet
Daily Charter	£120
Daily Individual	£18
Weekly Charter	£500 (5 days)
Tackle Hire	Shark and bottom outfits £3.50 daily; £16 weekly

Other boats available.

■ NOTABLE CAPTURES

Species	Weight	Location	Bait	Boat/Shore	Date
Bass	11 lbs 3 oz	Clonakilty	Razor Fish	S	10/90
Bass	10 lbs 1 oz	Ring Clonakilty	Crab	S	5/89
Bass	10 lbs 14½ oz	Rosscarbery	Peeler Crab	S	7/86
Bass	10 lbs 14 oz	Clonakilty	Sandeel	S	8/86
Bass	10 lbs ½ oz	Rosscarbery	Sandeel	S	10/86
Bass	11 lbs 13 oz	Clonakilty	Sandeel	S	8/85
Bass	10 lbs 8 oz	Ring Clonakilty	Sandeel	S	8/85
Bass	10 lbs 4 oz	Clonakilty Soft	Crab	S	6/84
Bass	16 lbs 3 oz	Ring Clonakilty	Sandeel	S	10/83
Flounder	3 lbs 1 oz	Ring Clonakilty	Peeler Crab	S	6/83
Mullet	6 lbs 14½ oz	Rosscarbery	Bread	S	9/91

■ IRISH RECORD

Scad	1.97	Clonakilty	Koster	S	9/86

COMMON SPECIES

Common Species	Average Size Caught (lbs)
Blue Shark	45
Conger	12
Pollack	7
Coalfish	3
Ling	10
Cod	5
Whiting	1.5
Ray	9
Dogfish	2
Pouting	1.5

TACKLE SHOPS

Kilty Lure Co. Ltd, Emmet Square, Clonakilty
Dave Spiller, General Merchant, 39 Pearse Street, Clonakilty

CLUBS AND CONTACTS

West Cork SAC, Catherine Lordan, Lakefield House,
Castlelack, Bandon, (021) 330138
Rosscarbery SAC, Tony O'Regan, 36 Newland Vale,
Rochestown Road, Douglas, Cork, (021) 891075

CONTACTS

Finbarr MacSweeney, The Kilty Lure Co. Ltd, Emmet Square,
Clonakilty, (023) 34377
Patrick Houlihan, 3/4 Connolly Street, Clonakilty, (023) 33654

COMPETITIONS

The two local clubs run many competitions throughout the
season. West Cork SAC is primarily a shore club and fishes the
beaches from Courtmacsherry to Baltimore. For further details,
contact club secretaries.

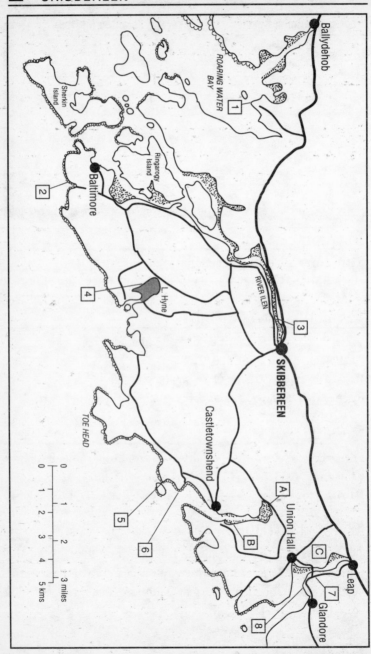

DESCRIPTION: SKIBBEREEN

The Skibbereen area is picturesque, full of inlets, creeks and rocky promontories. This diverse coastline encourages a wealth of marine animals to inhabit the area.

The main centre for boat angling is the village of Baltimore which is only 8 miles from Skibbereen. Deep sea angling offers a choice of Blue Shark angling, general fishing and wrecking. There are several wrecks within easy reach and these produce large Pollack, Ling and Conger.

Shore angling sites are still being uncovered almost annually, but most of the rock species are present, while the sandy beaches provide good Bass angling at times.

The boat season is normally from April to October, although wrecking trips can be made all year round. Shore fishing is from April to December.

SHORE ANGLING MARKS (map – page 116)

1. CASTLEVIEW: Bottom fishing from point for Flounder, Dogfish and occasional Bass. Low water to high water best. Also spinning for Sea Trout at high water.

2. TRAFRASKA: Spinning for Pollack and Mackerel at high water. Float fishing for Wrasse.

3. RIVER ILEN: Float fishing for Mullet at low water in channel beside main road upstream of bridge. Ground bait with bread flakes.

4. LOUGH HYNE: Unique fishing in very deep water from western shore under trees for Conger, Pollack, Mackerel, Wrasse, Gurnard and Dogfish. Float fishing for Mullet on northern side.

5. BEHIND HORSE ISLAND: Rock fishing in deep gully between mainland and island for Dogfish, Bull Huss, Coalfish, Conger, Pollack and Mackerel. High tide best. On left of channel occasional Ray taken at low water.

6. BATTERY POINT: Spinning and bottom fishing for Pollack, Flatfish and Dogfish at low water and the first of the flood.

7. ROAD BRIDGE: Fishing from bridge for Flounder, Dogfish and Bass. Crab and lugworm best baits. Float fishing for Mullet.

8. GLANDORE: Bottom fishing for Dogfish, Flatfish and occasional Bass. Best spot at point near main road.

■ BAIT (map – page 116)

A. RINEEN: Lugworm can be dug in upper reaches of estuary.

B. CASTLETOWNSHEND: Lugworm can be dug above pier on eastern shore.

C. UNION HALL: Good lugworm digging, below village. Also clam and mussel.

■ APPROVED BOATS FOR HIRE

Boat Name	Katsha	Cleona
Skipper/Owner	Michael Walsh Baltimore Marine Services Ltd, c/o Anglers Inn, Baltimore	Nick Dent Fastnet Charters, Ballydehob, Co. Cork
Base	Baltimore	Baltimore
Telephone	(028) 20145/20352/21300	(028) 37406/20143
Length	10.3 m (34 ft)	11 m (36 ft)
No. of Anglers	Shark–6-8; Bottom–8–10; Wreck–8	Shark–8 Ground/Wreck–10
Facilities	Echo Sounder, Radar, Navigator, 13–man Liferaft, Radio, Toilet	Radio, Sounder, Radar, Navigator, Life jackets, Toilet, Washing, Cooking, Liferaft
Daily Charter	£140 –8 persons (£100 minimum charge)	£100-£130 (£80 min charge)
Daily Individual	£20 max. per angler daily	By arrangement
Weekly Charter	£650 (5 days); £900 (7 days)	By arrangement
Tackle Hire	Shark outfit – £3 daily, £15 weekly. Bottom outfit– charge only for lost gear.	Free

Boat Name	Baltimore Oriel	Cliona's Wave
Skipper/Owner	Teddy Brown The Cove, Baltimore	Sean O'Brien Marine Hotel, Glandore, Co. Cork
Base	Baltimore	Glandore
Telephone	(028) 20319	(028) 33366; Fax 33600
Length	9.7 m (32 ft)	9.3 m (30½ ft)
No. of Anglers	Shark–6 Ground 6–8	Shark 6–8 Ground 6–8
Facilities	Echo Sounder, Radar, Navigator, Life saving equip. Radio, Toilet	Echo Sounder, Radar Navigator, Radio, Toilet, Life saving equip.
Daily Charter	£100 6–8 persons (£60 min charge)	£120
Daily Individual	£17	£15
Weekly Charter	£600 (7 days)	
Tackle Hire	Shark traces–£10, Rod Free; Bottom £5 daily; £30 weekly	No Rod Hire

■ CONTACTS

There are several other boats available for charter in the area.

NOTABLE CAPTURES

Species	Weight (lbs)	Location	Bait	Boat/Shore	Date
Bull Huss	20 lbs 3 oz	Baltimore	Mackerel	B	7/90
Lesser Spotted Dogfish	3.65	Union Hall	Mackerel	B	8/90
Blue Shark	129.0	Baltimore	Mackerel	B	8/90
Blue Shark	106.0	Baltimore	Mackerel	B	8/90
Conger	42.0	Baltimore	Mackerel	B	9/89
Pollack	14 lbs 13 oz	Union Hall	Eddystone	B	9/89
Blue Shark	102½	Fastnet	Mackerel	B	7/89
Ling	26.2 oz	Union Hall	Mackerel	B	5/89
Bull Huss	17.09	Union Hall	Mackerel	B	6/88
Coalfish	15.04 oz	Baltimore	Redgill	B	7/90
Ling	27.29	Baltimore	Mackerel	B	8/91

COMMON SPECIES

Common Species	Average Size Caught (lbs)
Blue Shark	45
Conger	15
Pollack	7
Coalfish	3
Ling	12
Cod	5
Whiting	1.5
Ray	8
Dogfish	2
Pouting	1.5

TACKLE SHOPS

Fallon Sports, 51 North Main Street, Skibbereen
Kilty Lure Co. Ltd, Emmet Square, Clonakilty
Dave Spiller, General Merchant, 39 Pearse Street, Clonakilty

CLUBS AND CONTACTS

Rosscarbery SAC, Tony O'Regan, 36 Newland Vale,
Rochestown Road, Douglas, Co. Cork (021) 891075
Schull SAC, Thomas Hanlon, Marine Bar, Schull, (028) 28455

■ COMPETITIONS

There are several competitions during the year. The main feature is the festival held in August at which visitors are welcome. For further details, contact Nick Dent (028) 37406 or Teddy Browne (028) 20319.

■ DESCRIPTION: MIZEN PENINSULA

On the rugged Mizen Peninsula are the towns of Ballydehob, Schull, Crookhaven and Durrus. The Mizen lighthouse, perched on the cliffs at the very tip of the 20–mile finger of land, is the most southerly point of the Irish mainland. The area is very scenic and unspoilt, with panoramic views out to the famous Fastnet light.

Boats operate out of Schull and Crookhaven and the general deep sea angling is excellent, with good catches of Blue Shark, Pollack, Cod, Ling, Bull Huss etc. 27 different species were recorded on rod and line here in one season fishing from Crookhaven.

Shore fishing offers a selection of venues such as beaches, piers and rocky headlands. Ray and Bull Huss are two of the species taken here, especially in August and September.

The boat angling season is from April to October and shore fishing continues up to December.

■ SHORE ANGLING MARKS (map – page 122)

1. TOUR PIER: Spinning for Pollack and Mackerel. Float fishing for Wrasse. Bottom fishing for Conger. High water best.
2. VAUD CREEK: Spinning from jetty for Coalfish, Pollack and Mackerel. Float fishing for Wrasse. Bottom fishing over mixed ground for Codling, Conger and occasional Plaice, Bass and Ray.

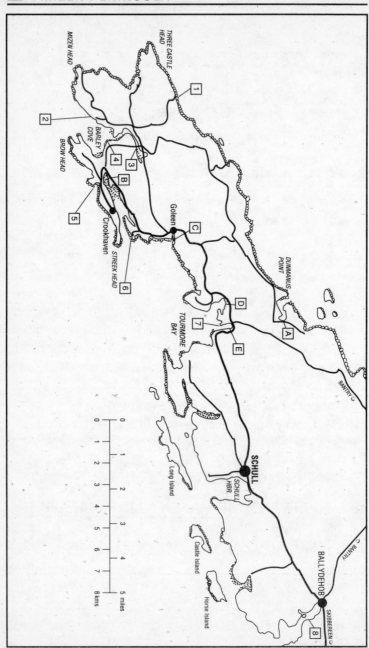

3. BARLEY LAKE: Bottom fishing from road bridge for Flounder, Freshwater Eel and Mullet (ground baiting essential). High water best. Spinning in channel for occasional Sea Trout. Flood tide at dusk most productive.

4. BARLEY COVE: Surf fishing from north and east beaches for Codling, Flounder, and occasional Bass, Dab and Plaice.

5. GALLEY COVE: Spinning from outer rocks for Pollack and Coalfish. Bottom fishing from inner rocks over mixed ground for Flounder, Dogfish, Bull Huss, Conger, Codling, small Turbot and Ray.

6. ROCK ISLAND: Rock fishing below lighthouse, over sand for Ray, Dab, Codling and Dogfish. Spinning for Pollack and Mackerel. Float fishing close to rocks for Wrasse. Flood tide best. Do not park in lighthouse grounds without permission.

7. TOURMORE: Fishing from rocks on both sides of channel for Wrasse, Dogfish, Bull Huss, Flounder and occasional Bass. Flood tide best.

8. BALLYDEHOB HARBOUR: Bottom fishing from rocks on eastern shore of island for Flounder and Bass and spinning for Sea Trout. Two hours either side of high water best.

■ BAIT (map – page 122)

A. DUNMANUS HARBOUR: Lugworm on southern shore, east of quay. Crab around base of quay.

B. CROOKHAVEN: Lugworm and occasional clam. Some crab around rocky outcrops.

C. GOLEEN: Lugworm in harbour and some crab north of slipway and around rocks.

D. TOURMORE WEST: Crab among weed on both sides of channel. Mussel on rocks.

E. ALTAR CHURCH: Lugworm and occasional clam on banks of channel. Crab around rocks. Clam at river mouth and lugworm north of pier.

■ APPROVED BOATS FOR HIRE

Boat Name	Jan Steen	Sea Angler
Skipper/Owner	Bear Havinga Crookhaven	Mike Roach Schull
Base	Crookhaven	Schull
Telephone	(028) 35240	(028) 37256
Length	11 m (36 ft)	8.3 m (28 ft)
No. of Anglers	Shark–4; Ground–4	Shark 4–6; Ground 6–8
Facilities	Echo Sounder, Radar, Navigator, Liferaft, Radio, Radar, Navigator, Life jackets	Echo Sounder, Radio, Life jackets, Toilet
Daily Charter	£60; £40 per half day 1 to 6 pm	£110
Daily Individual	£15	By arrangement
Weekly Charter	By arrangement	By arrangement
Tackle Hire	Included in price	Free

Other boats are available for competitions and weekends.

■ NOTABLE CAPTURES

Species	Weight (lbs)	Location	Bait	Boat/Shore	Date
Bull Huss	16.27	Schull	Squid	B	5/90
Pollack	13 lbs 14 oz	Crookhaven	Sandeel	B	4/90
Blue Shark	105.0	Crookhaven	Mackerel	B	8/90
Blue Shark	104.0	Schull	Mackerel	B	9/90
Blue Shark	105.0	Schull	Mackerel	B	7/89
Ling	25.16	Schull	Mackerel	B	9/88
Bull Huss	16.14 oz	Crookhaven	Mackerel	B	5/91

COMMON SPECIES

Common Species	Average Size Caught (lbs)
Blue Shark	45
Wrasse	3
Conger	12
Pollack	9
Coalfish	2
Ling	10
Cod	5
Whiting	1.5
Bull Huss	9
Ray	9
Turbot	6
Pouting	1

TACKLE SHOPS

Barnetts Hardware Shop, Main Street, Schull, Co. Cork
Fallons Sports, 51 North Street, Skibbereen, Co. Cork

CLUBS AND CONTACTS

Schull SAC, Thomas Hanlon, Marine Bar, Schull, Co. Cork,
(028) 28455
Contact, Brian Murphy, The Black Sheep Inn, Schull, Co. Cork
(028) 28203

COMPETITIONS

Schull SAC run many boat competitions throughout the season, including a Blue Shark Safari in August. For details, contact club secretary.

Bantry to the Ring of Kerry

This chapter covers a lot of shoreline, including three of the great peninsulas that are the main characteristic of the south-west. The Gulf Stream water is warm – and getting warmer, according to most climatologists. The fishing is very varied and the scenery is magnificent.

This is the part of Ireland where, every year, sub-tropical species stray northwards and there are reports of Flying Fish, Trigger Fish, Boar Fish, Puffer Fish and Sun Fish. It's also where pioneering anglers are trying to establish a rod and line fishery for Blue Fin Tuna. All this holds little direct interest for the angler at present, but there are plenty of commoner species that do.

Starting with Bantry Bay. This is a four-mile-wide finger of water of great depth, up to thirty fathoms, which stretches inland for twenty-one miles to the beauty spot of Glengarrif. It offers some good sheltered fishing for anglers who have their own dinghies or who fish from the shore. The main species is Whiting, which aren't usually associated with this sort of water. There is also Ray, Huss, Dogs, Flats, Conger, some Ling, and Spurdogs, which aren't as plentiful as they used to be. Spurdog, in fact, form one-half of an odd Irish Record double held by John Murnane. He caught the Irish record Spurdog in the bay in 1977 and came back in 1979 to add the Irish Record freshwater eel which he caught in a small lake called Droumenisa which is on Whiddy Island in the bay.

Shore anglers can find very good Ballan Wrasse and Pollack along the south shore and, over a patch of clean ground below the disused airfield at the east end, Ray, Huss, Dogs and Flats. There is some seasonal Sea Trout fishing in the streams that flow into the Bay.

The next peninsula up, the Beara Peninsula, is still very much off the beaten track where tourists are concerned and a lot of it is virgin territory for sea anglers. It's one of the few bits of the country where I've never even wetted a line myself. But I'm told there's rock, pier and some beach fishing. Wrasse and Pollack are the main species but there are Tope in Dursey Sound. I can certainly vouch for the fact that the scenery is spectacular.

The Kenmare River to the north of the peninsula isn't a river at all – it's a long saltwater bay with a Salmon river called the Roughty at the head of it. It's known for one angling oddity – it's probably the best place in the country to catch Slob Trout, an estuarine variety half way between Sea Trout and Brown Trout which is recognised as a separate category by the Irish Specimen Fish Committee.

There are a lot of aquaculture cages in this part of the world and Castletown Bearhaven on the southern coast of the peninsula is a major commercial fishing port. Accommodation on the Beara Peninsula may need a bit of pre-planning.

The Iveragh Peninsula is the next one up and it contains the famous Ring of Kerry, a tourist drive of over a hundred miles on small roads. If you attempt it, I suggest you follow the local convention and drive it in an anti-clockwise direction.

Sneem has an angling atmosphere. A lot of Dutch immigrants live in the area and some of them run charter boats. They have access to good fishing which, at times, becomes exceptional. This is really the base for big Spurdogs these days. They aren't a fish I enjoy catching, but if they turn you on go to Sneem. There's also a wealth of shore angling in the area against a great scenic backdrop. It's hard to pick out any particular hot spots, but the text of this chapter will direct you to what you're looking for.

Waterville also has an angling atmosphere, but the emphasis tends to be on the Salmon and large Sea Trout in Lough Currane and some of the rivers in the area. Sea angling takes something of a second place, but there are a number of charter boats in the area, though they aren't concentrated in any one centre.

Valentia, like Ballycotton in Co. Cork, played an important part in the history and development of sea angling as a sport around the turn of the century. It still provides big fish and a great variety of Atlantic species. There is also plenty of shore fishing on the island.

The Irish Specimen Fish Committee awards a special badge to any angler who has caught specimen fish of ten or more different species. Of the first three anglers who earned this badge, two were from Cahirciveen and one was a Dublin angler who always fished in Ballinskelligs. So there's no doubt that the blunt snout of the Iveragh Peninsula produces both quality and variety.

Glenbeigh on the peninsula's north coast offers a different kind of fishing over shallow, sandy ground, with quite good Bass and Flats from the shore and Tope from dinghies.

There's no coarse fishing in this part of the world, but the all-round angler will have no difficulty during spring, summer and autumn in getting access to good Salmon and Sea Trout fishing at a reasonable price. The Laune which drains the Killarney lakes to the tide at Killorglin is an excellent day ticket water for both species. Wild Brown Trout fishing is a bit harder for fish of any size, but it is possible by making local enquiries. The local Fisheries Board operates a number of excellent managed Rainbow/Brown Trout fisheries.

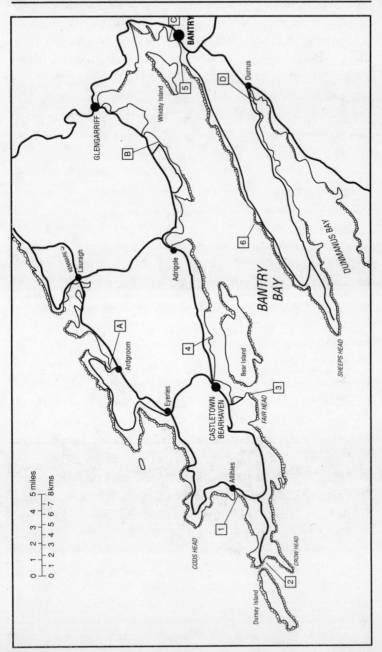

■ DESCRIPTION: BANTRY BAY

Bantry Bay is one of the deepest natural harbours in Europe, with depths exceeding 30 fathoms at the entrance between Sheep's Head and Bear Island. Only a limited amount of boat angling has taken place in recent years so a complete picture is not readily available.

However, shore fishing is popular, especially along the Dunmanus Peninsula and it is noted for its good fishing for Wrasse and Pollack. The Beara Peninsula also has some reasonable fishing marks such as Fair Head, Dursey and Ballydonegan and consists mainly of rock fishing for Conger, Wrasse, Pollack and Dogfish.

Small boat anglers can fish the waters near Bantry town for Ray, Bull Huss, Flatfish, Whiting, Codling and some Spurdog.

Season fished – April to October.

■ SHORE ANGLING MARKS (map – page 129)

1. BALLYDONEGAN: Bottom fishing for Bass and Flatfish on sandy beach at mouth of stream. Also bottom fishing from pier for Dogfish and Flatfish.
2. DURSEY SOUND: Good Wrasse fishing on north-western side of cable car. Also spinning for Pollack and Mackerel.
3. FAIR HEAD: A half mile walk from the end of the road takes you down to the point opposite lighthouse on Bear Island. Float and bottom fishing for Wrasse. Spinning for Pollack and Mackerel. Deep water towards channel.
4. D.O.D. PIER: Bottom fishing for Thornback Ray and Dogfish. Float fishing for Mullet. Ground bait is essential.
5. BEACH STRAND: Clean steep-to beach beside old airstrip. Good bottom fishing for Thornback Ray, Dogfish and Flatfish and some Bull Huss.
6. COLLACK: Float fishing for good size Wrasse; also some rocks where you can spin for Pollack.

■ BAIT (map – page 129)

A. ARDGROOM: Lugworm in sandy patches. Soft and peeler crab under weed near the pier.

B. ZETLAND PIER: Lugworm and some peeler crab below pier. Razor fish at low water springs.

C. COBH STRAND: Lugworm and some clams can be dug on beach. Mussels can also be collected.

D. DURRUS: Lugworm can be dug in muddy channels. Peeler and soft crab can be collected one mile from village.

■ APPROVED BOAT FOR HIRE

Boat Name	River Queen
Skipper/Owner	Michael O'Sullivan, Kenmare Holiday Cottages, Tuosist, Kenmare
Base	Lehid Harbour
Telephone	(066) 26323
Length	8 m (26 ft.)
No. of Anglers	Shark 4-6; Bottom 6-8
Facilities	Radio, Echo Sounder, Radar, Navigator, Liferaft, Toilet
Daily Charter	£160
Daily Individual	By arrangement
Weekly Charter	By arrangement
Tackle Hire	£2.50 daily

■ NOTABLE CAPTURES

Species	Weight (lbs)	Location	Bait	Boat/Shore	Date
Garfish	2¼	Bantry Bay	Feathers	B	8/89
Spurdog	18¾	Bantry Bay	Mackerel	B	9/77
Freshwater Eel	6 lbs 15 oz	Whiddy Island	Mackerel	S	6/79
Bull Huss	20	Bantry Bay	Mackerel	B	9/81
Wrasse	5	Dunmanus Peninsula	Lugworm	S	9/84

■ IRISH RECORD

Spurdog	18 lbs 12 oz	Bantry Bay	Mackerel	B	9/77

■ COMMON SPECIES

Common Species	Average Size Caught (lbs)
Conger	13
Spurdog	7
Ling	8
Pouting	1½
Bull Huss	9
Ballan Wrasse	3
Pollack	7
Ray	6

■ TACKLE SHOPS

O'Sullivans, Main Street, Castletown Bearhaven
Moriarty's, Main Street, Castletown Bearhaven

■ CLUBS AND CONTACTS

Bantry SAC, P. Ahern, Ardnagashel House, Bantry
Contact, Ramor Craige, Cametraingane House, Castletown
Bearhaven, (027) 70379/70390
Boat contact: Colm Harrington, Bear Island, (027) 75009

■ COMPETITIONS

For information on festivals and competitions, contact Ramor
Craige, (027) 70379.

■ DESCRIPTION: RING OF KERRY

The Waterville/Caherciveen area stretches from Sneem on the south-east of the Ring of Kerry to Glenbeigh on the north-west. It offers deep sea, shore and some inshore angling. Deep sea angling is carried out in deep water (30 to 50 fathoms) and offers a tremendous variety of species, including Blue Shark. There are several angling boats available scattered from Sneem to Valentia.

Shore fishing is comprised of estuary, beach, rock and pier marks. The main feature is the excellent rock hotspots, providing good angling for Pollack and Wrasse. This area also has some fine surf beaches which still provide some good angling for Bass and Flatfish.

Recent small boat fishing has produced good results for Codling, Whiting, Gurnard and Flatfish in Ballinskelligs Bay. The outer bay is consistent for large Pollack in excess of ten pounds.

The fishing season is from April to October for boat fishing, while the shore fishing extends to the end of November.

■ SHORE ANGLING MARKS (map – page 134)

1. ROSSBEHY CREEK: Spinning for Sea Trout. Bottom fishing on seaward side of gap in old causeway at Rossbehy Creek for Flounder and occasional Bass.
2. ROSSBEIGH: Surf fishing on beach and at point for Flatfish and occasional Bass. Occasional Tope and Ray in calm conditions.
3. LOUGH KAY: Beach fishing for Flatfish and occasional Ray.
4. VALENTIA HARBOUR: Bottom fishing for Ray and Conger. Float fishing for Mullet.
5. CULOO: Rock fishing for Pollack, Wrasse, Bull Huss, Conger, Dogfish and Mackerel.
6. ST FINIANS BAY: Surf fishing for Flounder, Dab and Bass.
7. INNY STRAND: Surf and beach fishing at river mouth and from main beach for Flatfish and Bass.

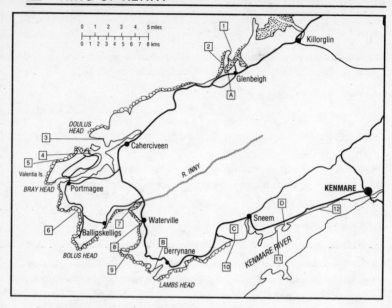

8. WATERVILLE: Beach fishing below car park for Flounder, Plaice, Dogfish and Bass.

9. HOGS HEAD: Rock fishing into deep water for Dab, Conger, Wrasse, Pollack, Codling and Mackerel.

10. GLEESK: Rock fishing for Wrasse, Pollack, Dogfish, Conger and occasional Ray.

11. OYSTERBED PIER: Bottom fishing for Conger, Ray, Wrasse and Mullet.

12. BLACKWATER HARBOUR: Bottom fishing and spinning for Ray, Conger, Pollack and Sea Trout from pier and rocks to the west.

BAIT

A. ROSSBEHY CREEK: Lugworm plentiful on seaward side of estuary.

B. DERRYNANE: Lugworm can be dug at southern end of Derrynane Harbour.

C. GLEESK: Some lugworm can be dug in harbour.

D. ROSSMORE ISLAND: Lugworm and clam can be dug between island and shore.

APPROVED BOATS FOR HIRE

Boat Name	An Chailleach Bhearra	Down Crest
Skipper/Owner	Aidan McAuliffe Locktar Cua, Waterville	Michael O'Sullivan Lobster Bar, Waterville,
Base	Derrynane (June to August)	Caherciveen
Telephone	(0667) 4519	(0667) 4255
Length	8 m (26 ft)	8.3 m (28 ft)
No. of Anglers	Shark–5; Bottom–6	Shark–4; Ground–6
Facilities	Radio, Echo Sounder, Radar, Navigator, Toilet, Life jackets	Radio, Echo Sounder, Radar, Navigator, Toilet, Life jackets, Liferaft, Washing, Cooking
Daily Charter	£100–6 persons (minimum charge £90)	£100–6 persons (minimum charge £70)
Daily Individual	£17-£20	£17-£20
Weekly Charter	£550 (6 days)	£550 (6 days)
Tackle Hire	Shark and bottom outfits– £5 daily; £30 weekly	Shark outfits £10 daily, £50 weekly; Bottom outfits – £6 daily, £35 weekly

Boat Name	Eagle II	Evening Star
Owner	Frank Murphy Foreign Exchange Co. of Ireland Ltd, Iveragh Rd	Paudie O'Shea Stone House, Sneem
Skipper	Tommy McGillycuddy (066) 61782	
Base	Killorglin	Sneem
Telephone	(066) 61258	(064) 45188/45332 (Cantharella Sports Motel)
Length	11.3 m (34 ft)	8.3 m (27 ft)
No. of Anglers	Shark–6; Ground 8–10	6–8
Facilities	Radio, Echo Sounder, Navigator, Toilet, Life jackets	Radio, Sounder, Radar Navigator, Life Jackets
Daily Charter	£300	By arrangement
Daily Individual	By arrangement	£15
Weekly Charter	By arrangement	By arrangement
Tackle Hire	Free	£3 daily

Boat Name	Christmas Eve	Naomh Crochan
Owner	Dan McCrohan Knightstown, Valentia Island, Co. Kerry	Sean O'Shea Bunavalla, Caherdaniel, Co. Kerry
Base	Valentia	Caherdaniel
Telephone	(0667) 6142	(0667) 5129
Length	9.1 m (30 ft)	9.1 m (30 ft)
No. of Anglers	Shark–5; Ground–7	Shark–6; Ground–6
Facilities	Radio, Echo Sounder, Radar, Navigator, Toilet, Life jackets, Washing, Cooking	Radio, Echo Sounder, Navigator, Toilet, Life jackets, Cooking
Daily Charter	£100–6 persons; £120–shark fishing	£130 (6 persons)
Daily Individual	£20	By arrangement
Weekly Charter	By arrangement	£500
Tackle Hire	Check beforehand	Shark and Bottom outfits– £5 daily; £24 weekly

Boat Name	L'Oursin
Owner	Sean O'Shea Bunavalla, Caherdaniel, Co. Kerry
Base	Caherdaniel
Telephone	(0667) 5129
Length	9.8 m (32 ft)
No. of Anglers	Shark–8; Ground–8
Facilities	Radio, Echo Sounder, Navigator, Toilet, Life jackets, Washing, Cooking
Daily Charter	£130–8 persons
Daily Individual	By arrangement
Weekly Charter	£500–6 days
Tackle Hire	Shark and Bottom outfits– £5 daily; £24 weekly

Other boats are available for charter and competitions.

■ NOTABLE CAPTURES

Species	Weight (lbs)	Location	Bait	Boat/Shore	Date
Bull Huss	16.5	Sneem	Mackerel	B	6/91
Spur Dogfish	13.0	Sneem	Mackerel	B	7/91
Grey Gurnard	.707 kg	Skelligs	Mackerel	B	6/90
Plaice	4 lbs 7¾ oz	Ballinskelligs	Lugworm	S	7/90
Pouting	3.2	Valentia	Mackerel	B	8/90
Grey Mullet	5 lbs 1 oz	Waterville	Lugworm	S	10/89
Tope	41.0	Kenmare	Mackerel	B	9/89
Conger	40.2	Kenmare	Squid	B	9/89
Ballan Wrasse	4.86	Sneem	Shrimp	B	9/89

■ IRISH RECORDS

Species	Weight (lbs)	Location	Bait	Boat/Shore	Date
Conger	72.0	Valentia	Mackerel	B	1914
Rays Bream	6 lbs 6¼ oz	Valentia	Pirk	B	8/78
Red Sea Bream	9.6	Valentia	Feathers	B	8/63
Whiting	4 lbs 14½ oz	Kenmare	Mackerel	B	3/81
Bull Huss	23.12	Valentia	Mackerel	B	5/83
Lesser Spotted Dogfish	4.4	Valentia	Mackerel	B	7/82

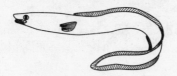

COMMON SPECIES

Common Species	Average Size Caught (lbs)
Blue Shark	45
Pollack	7
Coalfish	4.5
Ling	11
Conger	14
Ray	7
Tope	25
Cod	5
Bull Huss	9
Dogfish	2

TACKLE SHOPS

Paddy McGuire, Anchor Bar, Main Street, Caherciveen
Anglers Rest, Waterville
Landers Tackle Shop, Courthouse Lane, Tralee

CLUBS AND CONTACTS

Caherciveen SAC, Michael Quinlan, c/o Kerry Fish Ltd, Renard, Caherciveen, (0667) 2177
Killarney SAC, Richard Behal, 85 Woodlawn Park, Killarney, Co. Kerry, (064) 32723
Kells Bay SAC, Gerard O'Sullivan, Mountain Stage, Glenbeigh, Co. Kerry

CONTACTS

Michael O'Driscoll, Cive Minerals, Caherciveen, (0667) 2065
Michael O'Sullivan, Lobster Bar, Waterville, (0667) 4255
IRD Waterville, (0667) 4366

COMPETITIONS

The two main competitions, which are annual events, are the International Boat Festival in early August and the Open Shore Match in October. Further details from Michael Quinlan, (0667) 2177

Dingle Peninsula & Fenit

INTRODUCTION

I think I've done more sea angling on the Dingle Peninsula than anywhere else in the west of Ireland. I've been going down there for over twenty years simply because it's one of my favourite parts of the country. But it's hard to sit down and analyse exactly why you like a place. It's such a combination of things – great scenery, great pubs, great people – and, of course, the fishing.

When I first started to go down in the early seventies, it was all about Bass. Dingle had the most famous surf beaches in Europe and they were dotted with angling pilgrims from all over, in chest waders, concentrating hard on what was happening the far side of the third breaker. Then the Bass declined because of heavy commercial fishing pressure and we started to turn our attention to other species like Flounder, Wrasse and Tope. Today, there are some signs that the Bass are making a slow come-back under the protection of the new legislation and will again play a part in the mixed sea angling of an extraordinary peninsula.

Dingle is a self-contained entity, thirty-five miles long by fifteen miles wide. It has a backbone of mountains provided by the Slieve Mish and Ireland's second highest peak in Mount Brandon. There are spectacular cliffs facing the Atlantic, offshore islands, several very sheltered natural harbours and two magnificent tombolas. A tombola, as I only discovered recently, is a geographers' term for a peninsula of sand dunes with a storm beach facing the Atlantic. The one on the south side of Dingle is called Inch and the one on the north side the Maharees. They provide the finest of the Bass beaches.

But Dingle has several other very important assets for the sea angler. First of all, its geography is such that it's possible to find calm water to fish from the shore or a dinghy even in a hurricane. At the other extreme, you can find a Bass surf even in a flat calm. Then it has an enormous variety of fishing. The quality of the beaches should not overshadow the fact that it has some of the best Wrasse holes in Ireland. It has also been developed for match fishing. And finally, Dingle town is an important commercial fishing harbour with a fish processing plant, a good supply of bait and tackle, and good charter boat operators with access to everything from shallow, sandy ground for Tope to pinnacle rocks out around the Blasket Islands.

Dingle offers everything from Shark to excellent Mullet and, as if that wasn't enough, some of the best Brown Trout fishing in Kerry in Lough Gill, about the second best in Mount Eagle lake. There is some good fishing for Sea Trout and occasional Salmon in a number of small streams and lakes if you are lucky enough to be in the right place at exactly the right time.

The peninsula is bounded on the north by Tralee Bay and the angling centre for the bay is Fenit, though the town of Tralee also has some excellent tackle shops. Fenit too is an exceptional place and an ideal base for a holiday where it's possible to enjoy weeks of varied boat, shore and pier fishing without ever having to drive a car.

Fenit is dominated by one of the finest piers in Ireland which stretches out into deep water. From different points along the pier you can expect to catch different types of fish — Ray, Conger, Pollack, Flats and Dogs; even Monks and Common Skate have been taken! In fact, there is access to so much water from the pier that it really amounts to boat fishing for bad sailors.

The conventional shore fishing in the area is excellent. It's probably the best bit of water around Ireland for Turbot from the shore. The angler who's interested in adding to his tally of species should note that six species of Ray are taken and it is, for practical purposes, the only place in Ireland where you can catch Undulate Ray.

One of the most pleasant aspects of the charter boat fishing out of Fenit is the short steaming time to the marks. Fifteen minutes after casting off, you can be over probably the best Monkfish grounds in Ireland, with plenty of Tope, Dogfish and Ray.

Angling in Fenit has a long history, but there's no doubt that the big growth area at present is in owner-operated dinghies. This is my favourite form of sea angling and Tralee Bay is an excellent place to practise it, provided you accept that it is somewhat open to westerly winds and can develop a heavy sea quite rapidly.

Conservation and tagging are a big thing in this area. The bulk of fish caught are released unharmed and there is probably a higher density of tagged fish than anywhere else around our coast.

Yes, I think I'd have to admit that if the great god of angling informed me one day that, for the rest of my life, I had to restrict my sea angling to the waters covered by only one chapter of this book, I'd opt for this one.

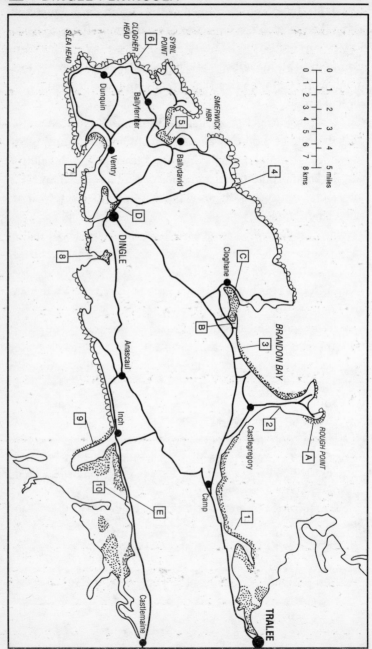

SLEA HEAD
CLOGHER HEAD
SYBIL POINT

6

Dunquin
Ballyferriter

5

SMERWICK HBR

7

Ventry
Ballydavid

4

D

DINGLE

Cloghane

C

8

B

3

Anascaul

BRANDON BAY

9

Inch

2

Castlegregory

A

ROUGH POINT

10

E

Camp

1

Castlemaine

TRALEE

DESCRIPTION: THE DINGLE PENINSULA

The Dingle Peninsula is the most northerly of the five fingers of land jutting out into the Atlantic from the south-west corner of Ireland. It is 35 miles in length and varies from 8 to 15 miles in width. The scenery here is superb, with magnificent beaches interspersed with rocky headlands and cliffs.

For almost half a century, the Dingle Peninsula has been synonymous with white-water surf fishing for Bass. Although they are not as common as in years gone by, Bass can still be encountered for much of the year. Other species which were once overshadowed are now receiving much more attention.

For instance, the rock marks are capable of producing some of the best Wrasse fishing in Ireland. Ray, Pollack and Conger are also quite numerous. Boat fishing can also be exceptional, with Tope fishing particularly good. Excellent sport is also available with the Pollack and Coalfish which are plentiful around the Blaskets.

Boat fishing is from April to October and shore fishing on the surf beaches is practised well into December.

SHORE ANGLING MARKS (map – page 142)

1. DERRYMORE: Surf fishing. Flatfish, Ray and occasional Bass on beach. Bottom fishing for Flatfish, Ray and occasional Bass from point.
2. CASTLEGREGORY: Beach fishing for Flounder, Dogfish and occasional Bass near stream. Distance casting from car park, above landfill, for Ray (Thornback, Painted and Sting Ray recorded), Dogfish, Bull Huss, Plaice and Conger.
3. BRANDON BAY: Surf fishing all along beach for Flatfish and Bass. Ray in calm, warm weather. Flounder and Bass from estuary at Cloghane.
4. BRANDON CREEK: Fishing from rocks on eastern shore for Conger, Wrasse, Dogfish, Pollack and Bull Huss. Spinning for Mackerel.

5. SMERWICK HARBOUR: Surf fishing for Flounder, Bass, Coalfish and occasional Codling on Ballinrannig Strand.

6. CLOGHER HEAD TO SLEA HEAD: Wrasse fishing from northern side of Clogher Head, below 'Ryan's Daughter' schoolhouse and under grotto on Slea Head. Spinning for Pollack, Mackerel and Coalfish. Bottom fishing over very foul ground for Conger, Bull Huss and Dogfish.

7. VENTRY STRAND: Beach fishing for Dogfish, Flounder, Wrasse (in weed margins), Conger, Bull Huss and occasional Bass in surf.

8. TRABEG: Surf fishing for Bass, Flounder, Dab, occasional Mullet and Dogfish. Ray in calm conditions.

9. INCH: Surf fishing for Bass, Flounder and Dabs. Dogfish and occasional Ray in calm conditions.

10. BACK OF INCH: Bottom fishing for Flounder, Plaice, some Bass and occasional Turbot. Flooding tide best using crab.

■ BAIT (map – page 142)

A. KILSHANNIG: Lugworm plentiful. Some crab can be collected on rock outcrops.

B, C. CLOGHANE ESTUARY: Lugworm and some white ragworm behind Fermoyle Strand. Crab along banks of channel at Cloghane.

D. MILLTOWN: Lugworm and clam at low-water mark below road.

E. CASTLEMAINE HARBOUR: Lugworm in mud behind Inch Strand and below road to Castlemaine. Some crab in patches of weed.

■ APPROVED BOATS FOR HIRE

Boat Name	Cashen Heather	Rod 'n' Reel	Lady Avalon
Skipper/Owner	John Young The Curlews, Lower Tier, Brandon, Tralee	George Burgum Dingle Bay Angling Centre Beenbawn, Dingle	Nicholas O'Conner Anglers Rest, Angling Centre Ventry, Dingle
Base	Brandon Pier	Dingle Pier	Dingle
Telephone	(066) 38264	(066) 51337	(066) 59947
Length	10.3 m (34 ft)	9.4 m (31 ft)	9.1 m (30 ft)
No. of Anglers	Shark 6–8 Bottom–8	Shark–8 Bottom–10; Wreck–10	Shark–8 Ground–12 Wreck–8
Facilities	Navigator, Radar, Radio, Echo Sounder, Toilet, Life jackets	Echo Sounder, Radio, Radar, Navigator, Toilet, 2 6–man Liferafts	Echo Sounder, Radio, Navigator, Liferaft, Toilet
Daily Charter	£130	£150 (min charge £100)	£150 (min charge £100)
Daily Individual	£20	£25	£25
Weekly Charter	£910	£1000	By arrangement
Tackle Hire	£3 daily	£3–daily Shark and bottom outfits– £3 daily; £20 weekly	Bottom outfits– £5 daily; Shark outfit–£10

■ NOTABLE CAPTURES

Species	Weight (lbs)	Location	Bait	Boat/Shore	Date
Pollack	12.15	Dingle	Redgill	B	5/91
Ballan Wrasse	2.5 kg	Dingle	Crab	S	9/90
Ballan Wrasse	2.340 kg	Ballyferriter	Crab	S	9/90
Bass	10 lbs 7¼ oz	Formoyle	Lugworm	S	4/90
Pouting	3.23	Dingle	Mackerel	B	9/89
Flounder	3 lbs 3 oz	Ballyferriter	Peeler Crab	S	9/89
Grey Mullet	5 lbs 4 oz	Brandon Bay	Mackerel	S	9/89
Painted Ray	14.0	Brandon Bay	Mackerel	B	9/88
Bull Huss	16.0	Dingle Bay	Mackerel	B	7/87
Sting Ray	30.5	Castlegregory	Sandeel	S	9/87

■ IRISH RECORD

| Ballan Wrasse | 4.3 kg | Clogher Head | Lugworm | S | 8/83 |

■ COMMON SPECIES

Common Species	Average Size Caught (lbs)
Coalfish	2.75
Cod	4.75
Conger	13
Dab	.5
Spurdog	7.5
Lesser Spotted Dogfish	2.5
Bull Huss	10.75
Ling	9.5
Plaice	1.75
Pollack	7
Thornback Ray	7
Blue Shark	45
Tope	31.75
Whiting	2

■ TACKLE SHOPS

Fitzgeralds Hardware, Dingle Town
Walter Sheehy, near the Pier, Dingle Town
Landers, Courthouse Lane, Tralee

■ CLUBS AND CONTACTS

There are no angling clubs in Dingle.
Contacts:
George Burgum, Beenbawn, Dingle, (066) 51337
John Young, Lower Tier, Brandon, (066) 38264
Maurice Fitzgerald, Grocery, Castlegregory, (066) 39133

■ COMPETITIONS

Since 1981, the Dingle Pairs has been held in Dingle in
September and October.

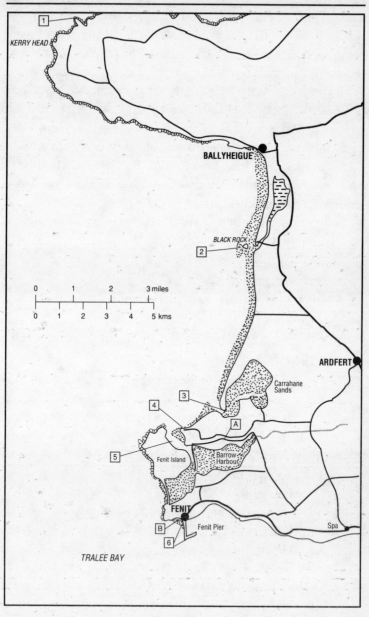

KERRY HEAD

1

BALLYHEIGUE

BLACK ROCK

2

0   1   2   3 miles

0   1   2   3   4   5 kms

ARDFERT

Carrahane
Sands

3

A

4

5   Fenit Island

Barrow
Harbour

FENIT

B   Fenit Pier

6   Spa

TRALEE BAY

■ DESCRIPTION: FENIT

The village of Fenit lies about 8 miles from Tralee on the northern shore of Tralee Bay. Fenit has for many years been a very popular angling centre. Apart from the excellent boat fishing in the bay, shore fishing in this area is equally good and Fenit Pier is one of the finest in the south of Ireland. Tralee Bay is renowned for its Tope and Monk fishing. As well as this, six species of Ray are captured here, including Homelyn, Sting and Undulate. Common Skate are also taken here each year.

Shore species include Ray, Flatfish, Bass, Pollack, Bull Huss and Dogfish. Monkfish and Common Skate have been recorded by shore anglers from Fenit Pier.

Boat angling is from April to October and shore angling continues right through to December.

■ SHORE ANGLING MARKS (map – page 147)

1. KERRY HEAD: Float fishing and bottom fishing from various rock ledges for Wrasse to specimen size, Pollack, Bull Huss, Dogfish and Conger.

2. BANNA STRAND: Spinning from rocks on seaward side of Black Rock for Bass, last of ebb to early flood. Bottom fishing to north-east of rock at high water for Flounder, small Turbot and Bass. Surf fishing south of rock, on beach for Flounder, Dab, small Turbot and Bass. Occasional Ray and Dogfish in calm weather.

3. CARRAHANE CHANNEL: Bottom fishing for Flounder, small Turbot, Bass and occasional Ray and Tope at Poll Gorm (Blue Pool). Flounder and Bass (surf fishing) from beach on flood tide.

4. BARROW HARBOUR: Bottom fishing for Dogfish, Flounder, Bass and occasional Tope. Spinning for Bass late ebb to early flood. Fishing from rocks at round castle for Flounder, Turbot, Bass and occasional Ray.

5. FENIT ISLAND: Bottom fishing for Bass (specimen fish recorded), Flounder and occasional Tope. Spinning produces Bass on a flood tide. Late ebb to early flood best.

6. FENIT PIER: Bottom fishing from viaduct for Dogfish, Flatfish, Ray and some Bass. Conger and small Pollack from rocks on seaward side of viaduct. Bottom fishing for Dogfish, Flatfish, Ray, Whiting and Conger at extreme end and seaward side. Occasional Tope, Monkfish and Common Skate have also been taken. Mullet fishing at high water on inside of pier using small pieces of fish offal.

■ BAIT (map – page 147)

A. BARROW HARBOUR: Lugworm can be dug on northern side of channel. Some crab can be collected under seaweed.

B. PIER BEACH: Sandeel and some lugworm on low water springs.

■ APPROVED BOATS FOR HIRE

Boat Name	Fin Ron	Oceaneering
Skipper/Owner	Michael Moriarty Talaught, Fenit	John Deady, 12 Castleview, Fenit
Base	Fenit Pier	Fenit Pier
Telephone	(066) 36303	c/o Michael Godley (066) 36108
Length	8 m (26 ft)	8.3 m (27 ft)
No. of Anglers	Shark–6; Ground–8	Ground— 5–6
Facilities	Echo Sounder, Radio, Navigator, Toilet, Life jackets,	Sounder, Radio, Life jackets, Toilet
Daily Charter	£80	£80
Daily Individual	By arrangement	By arrangement
Weekly Charter	By arrangement	By arrangement
Tackle Hire	£5 daily	£4-5 daily

Many other boats available for competitions at weekends.

NOTABLE CAPTURES

Species	Weight (lbs)	Location	Bait	Boat/Shore	Date
Monkfish	60	Tralee Bay	Mackerel	B	7/90
Monkfish	59	Tralee Bay	Mackerel	B	7/90
Sting Ray	47	Tralee Bay	Mackerel	B	5/90
Painted Ray	10 lbs 4 oz	Tralee Bay	Squid	B	10/89
Pollack	12 lbs 7 oz	Maherees	Baited Feathers	B	7/89
Monkfish	63	Fenit	Mackerel	B	5/89
Undulate Ray	15 lbs 1 oz	Fenit	Squid	B	6/88
Sting Ray	46 lbs 2 oz	Fenit	Peeler Crab	S	9/88
Common Skate	160 (returned alive)	Fenit	Mackerel	B	7/88

IRISH RECORDS

Species	Weight (lbs)	Location	Bait	Boat/Shore	Date
Monkfish	73	Fenit	Mackerel	B	6/80
Sting Ray	51	Fenit	Mackerel	S	8/70
Undulate Ray	18	Fenit	Mackerel	B	6/77

COMMON SPECIES

Common Species	Average Size Caught (lbs)
Cod	3.5
Conger	7.5
Dab	.5
Spurdog	7.5
Lesser Spotted Dog	1.75
Bull Huss	7.5
Grey Gurnard	.75
Monkfish	39
Tope	30
Thornback Ray	6
Sting Ray	21.75
Undulate Ray	8.25

TACKLE SHOPS

Landers, Courthouse Lane, Tralee
Benners, Bridge Street, Tralee

CLUBS AND CONTACTS

Tralee Bay SAC, Ruth Kelter, 25 Shanakill, Monavalley, Tralee,
(066) 25935
Kingdom SAC, Blanche Rutland, 34 Casements View, Ardfert,
Tralee
Boat contact, Michael Godley, Godley's Hotel, Fenit,
(066) 36108

COMPETITIONS

There are numerous shore and boat competitions held in
Tralee Bay. For further details, contact club secretaries.

Shannon Estuary & Co. Clare

INTRODUCTION

The next great inlet of the sea as one goes northwards up the west coast is the Shannon Estuary. It's a very different proposition to Tralee Bay, but an interesting one nonetheless.

Very little was known about the sea angling potential of the area until quite recently when research work by the Central Fisheries Board and Limerick-based angling clubs came up with some interesting results.

The main thing that makes the Shannon Estuary different from the other great inlets along the west coast is a powerful run of tide – up to four knots in the main channel. Most of the fishing is from dinghies and the secret of success is to avoid this tide. It's not so much the fact that it makes fishing difficult or even dangerous, as that the fish seem to have worked out the slack spots of the current and tend to congregate in them.

Finding these spots is partly a matter of common sense. But the tidal currents are complex in the estuary and one good tip is to get an admiralty chart. You'll find little anchor symbols on the chart which mark places where the old sailing ship skippers used to anchor while they waited for wind and tide. They almost invariably provide good and comfortable fishing. And the plus side of the whole thing for dinghy skippers is that there's great weather shelter in the estuary, much better than in Tralee Bay, and wind and sea conditions are much less likely to interfere with angling.

The fishing is almost exclusively for the species that suffer from the derogatory title of 'animals'. There are quality Huss and Thornbacks, good Tope in season, Dogs and Conger. The survey work has concentrated on the area between Foynes and Carrigaholt. The eastern end of the estuary may hold some surprises, including Flats and Bass.

Shore fishing is a matter of using common sense to pick a mark away from the mudflats where an outcrop of some kind gives you access to deeper water. Some of these can be quite good. The shore bait is crab, which is fairly easy to collect. The boat bait is Mackerel and can pose problems as there's little commercial fishing in the area. If you are reduced to frozen Mackerel, try and get it blast frozen rather than from a normal freezer.

The new charter boat operation at Kilrush fishes the estuary as well as offshore marks. There is a passenger and car ferry between Killimer and Tarbert.

The scenery of the estuary is a matter of taste. I rather like the backdrop of rolling hills, the islands and the large number of castle ruins. I don't even object to the factories and power stations that punctuate the skyline and the commercial shipping that uses the channel. I was down there recently and I came away saying: 'This is a bit of the coast I must get to know better'.

The rest of Co. Clare divides naturally into two parts – the Atlantic coast of South Clare and the limestone country of North Clare. South Clare, particularly the stretch of cliffs between Loop Head and Kilkee, is not, for my money, the most interesting stretch of coastline in Ireland for the sea angler. The

Blue Pool north of Kilkee is a popular rock mark offering access to deep water, but it's also a tragic one. So far it has drowned ten anglers. The local authority has blasted away the cliff path access in an attempt to stop this recurring, but anglers, often equipped with ropes and climbing gear, still go down for Wrasse, Pollack, Mackerel and other species.

Farther north again, access gets much easier at Doughmore and there is fishing for Dogfish, Ray Bass and Flats. But the next point of real interest is Green Island because it, along with Ballyreen, was the scene of exploits of one of Ireland's most amazing sea anglers. In the early 1960s, Jack Shine, a local man, set himself the apparently impossible task of catching Porbeagle Shark, our largest angling species, from the shore. Despite tackle which was very primitive by today's standards, he eventually succeeded, landing several fish over a hundred pounds in weight. It was an amazing feat and only happened because Jack devoted huge amounts of time, effort and angling genius to the project. Given his sort of dedication, it could probably be done again.

Lahinch is a resort town, not easy to fish on a sunny Sunday, but you can usually get away from the crowds by walking up north of the river. There are Bass and Flats, and Salmon run the river. There's a boat in Liscannor, but the next stretch of coast is the Cliffs of Moher. If you walk to the edge, you'll find you haven't enough line on your reel to reach the water.

There's another boat in Doolin which can fish out around the Aran Islands. But the high point of Clare shore angling is certainly the great limestone platforms around Black Head where the Burren meets the sea. This is world-class rock fishing, well publicised and home to the World Rock Fishing Championships. It's as comfortable, easy and safe as rock fishing ever is. There are signposts and the rocks are even numbered for the match anglers. When you're ready to cast, you have two distinct choices. You can either fish in the rough ground at your feet for Wrasse, Pollack, Conger and Rockling, or you can hurl your bait out sixty yards plus onto cleaner ground in deep water and get big Ray and Huss, Dogs and Flats.

Round the corner on the south shore of Galway Bay there is an angling and holiday centre in Ballyvaughan, and some interesting and sheltered water with little tidal creeks up around New Quay and Kinvara.

Clare is, in fact, a popular county for holidaymakers from home and abroad. They come for the traditional music, the plant life of the Burren, the pubs and angling. But when I read about how we are trying to develop 'activity holidays' in this country and what an important role angling is going to play in all this, I sometimes think the planners should come to Co. Clare and take a close look at the holidaymakers. Many of them, it seems to me, are coming for *in*–activity holidays. They seem to be quite happy to be in Clare doing absolutely nothing!

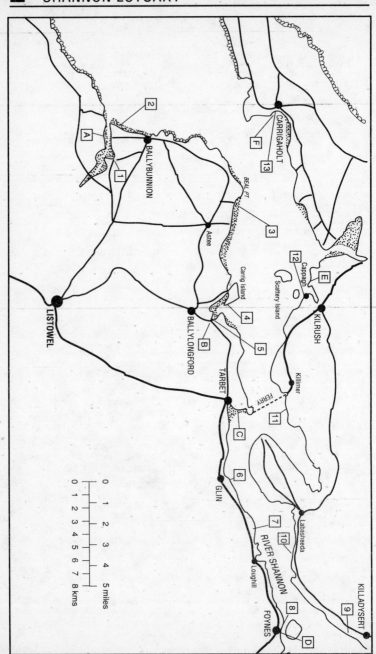

◾ DESCRIPTION: SHANNON ESTUARY

The lower half of the Shannon Estuary runs into the Atlantic Ocean between Co. Clare in the north and counties Limerick and Kerry in the south. Angling activity is a comparatively new phenomenon in this region and the early results are very promising.

It is an excellent venue for small boat anglers, although larger charter boats can also enjoy the good fishing for Tope, Bull Huss, Thornback Ray, Dogfish and some Conger. In windy conditions, anglers can select and enjoy comfortable sheltered bays, getting the maximum time afloat. The quality of the Tope fishing is first class and, together with numerous Bull Huss and Ray, ensures plenty of activity.

Wherever shore anglers have access to deep water from piers or rocky outcrops, good results can be expected. Ray, Bull Huss, Conger and Flatfish are taken on a regular basis and even an occasional Tope has been landed from the shore, especially around the Kilteery Pier area.

The season for Tope is late June to September. For all other species it is April to October. Shore anglers can fish right up to December, expecting catches of Codling, Whiting and Flatfish.

◾ SHORE ANGLING MARKS (map – page 156)

1. CASHEN ESTUARY: Bottom fishing below car park for numerous Flounder and occasional Bass. Best at low water through to high water. Crab is the most productive bait.
2. BALLYBUNION BEACH: Beach and surf fishing on northern side of Cashen Estuary for Bass and Flounder. Flooding tide best.
3. LITTOR STRAND: Bottom fishing for Dogfish, Bull Huss and Flatfish. Best stage of the tide is low water to half flood.
4. CARRIG ISLAND: Cross the bridge and turn right. Follow (on foot) track through fields to the south-east point of island. Bottom fishing in muddy channel for Bull Huss, Thornback Ray, Dogfish and Flounder. Can fish at all stages of the tide.

5. SALEENS: Good bottom fishing for Flounder from quay. Crab bait essential. Fish the flooding tide.

6. GLIN: Park in layby on Foynes side of Glin village. Good bottom fishing from beach on flooding tide for Bull Huss, Ray, Dogfish, Conger and Flatfish.

7. KILTEERY PIER: This is an excellent mark on the flooding tide to high water for Thornback Ray, Bull Huss, Dogfish, Dab, Plaice, Flounder and small Conger. Occasional Smooth Hounds at night.

8. FOYNES: Bottom fishing on beach below swimming pool into deep channel for Thornback Ray, Dogfish and Codling. Small Conger at night. Crab best bait. Flooding tide to high water. Whiting and Flounder taken from piers.

9. NEW QUAY: Bottom fishing from jetty on left-hand side for Bull Huss, Ray, Conger, Dogfish and freshwater Eel.

10. AILLROE: Bottom fishing from rocks near main road for Thornback Ray, Bull Huss, Dogfish and Conger.

11. KILLIMER: Bottom fishing on beach on left-hand side of ferry terminal for Bull Huss, Ray, Conger and Dogfish.

12. CAPPAGH PIER: Bottom fishing from end of pier for Bull Huss, Dogfish, Conger, Whiting and some Ray.

13. CARRIGAHOLT: Fishing from pier for Dab, Flounder and Dogfish. Spinning and float fishing for Pollack and Wrasse. Night fishing for Conger.

■ BAIT (map – page 156)

A. CASHEN ESTUARY: Lugworm are plentiful on south side of estuary inside pier. Some soft and peeler crab under weedy patches on north side.

B. SALEEN JETTY: Soft and peeler crab can be gathered on beach downstream from jetty.

C. TARBERT: Halfway between Tarbert village and the ferry pier brings you to a seaweed-covered point. This is an excellent site for collecting soft and peeler crab in season.

D. FOYNES: Some soft and peeler crab can be collected on the beach west of the swimming pool at low water.

E. KILRUSH: Excellent lugworm here which must be dug at low water. Some peeler crab under weedy ridges. This beach is located by taking first turn left at Kilrush graveyard.

F. CARRIGAHOLT: Soft and peeler crab can be collected near the pier. Some lugworm and small white ragworm beside inner pier.

■ APPROVED BOATS FOR HIRE

Boat Name	Gabhlan Gaoithe, Crosán & Guardal	Karen Ann
Skipper/Owner	Michael McLaughlin Atlantic Adventures, Frances Street, Kilrush	Martin Brennan 4 Kilkee Road, Kilrush, Co. Clare
Base	Kilrush	Kilrush
Telephone	(065) 52133	(065) 52031
Length	10.5 m (35 ft)	9.1 m (30 ft)
No. of Anglers	Shark–8, Bottom–10	Shark 6–8; Bottom 8–10
Facilities	Echo Sounder, Radio, Navigator, Liferaft, Toilet	Echo Sounder, Radio, Navigator, Liferaft, Toilet
Daily Charter	£225 (10 persons) (min. charge £150)	£100 (min. charge £70)
Daily Individual	£25	£13
Weekly Charter	£1200 – 6 days	By arrangement
Tackle Hire	£5 daily; £30 weekly	£4

3 Self Drive Boats, 2 Outboard (17 feet) and 1 Inboard Diesel (18 feet) can be hired at Kilrush. Contact is Michael McLaughlin, Atlantic Adventures, Frances Street, Kilrush, Tel (065) 52133.

■ NOTABLE CAPTURES

Species	Weight (lbs)	Location	Bait	Boat/Shore	Date
Bull Huss	15	Clonderalaw Bay	Mackerel	B	7/90
Thornback Ray	14	Clonderalaw Bay	Mackerel	B	7/90
Tope	35	Carrig Island	Mackerel	B	8/90
Conger	25	Clonderalaw Bay	Mackerel	B	6/90
Bull Huss	15	Auginish Jetty	Crab	S	8/90

COMMON SPECIES

Common Species	Average Size Caught (lbs)
Tope	25
Bull Huss	10
Dogfish	1.75
Thornback Ray	8
Codling	2
Conger	6
Plaice	1
Dab	.75
Whiting	1

TACKLE SHOPS

Jim Robinson, Thomond Shopping Centre, Roxboro, Limerick, (061) 44900

Atlantic Adventures, Frances Street, Kilrush (065) 52133

Michael O'Sullivan, Moore Street, Kilrush

CLUBS AND CONTACTS

Limerick SAC, Dave McCarthy, 91 Bouldavoher Estate, Limerick (061) 28745

West Clare SAC, Jacqueline Darcy, 4 Cappagh Drive, Kilrush

Shannon Town SAC, Tom Baracry, 1 Tolka Park, Shannon

Contact, Jim Robinson, Robinson's Tackle Shop, Thomond Shopping Centre, Roxboro, Limerick, (061) 44900

COMPETITIONS

There are two annual competitions to note. These are the Inter-firm held in May and the small inshore boat festival held at Kilrush in early June. For further details, contact Jim Robinson, Robinson's Tackle Shop, Limerick (061) 44900.

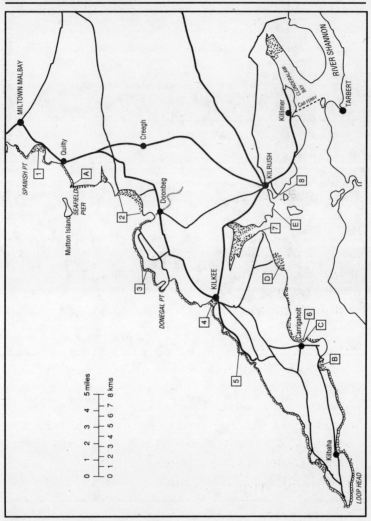

■ DESCRIPTION: SOUTH CLARE

The coastline of South Clare stretches from Liscannor Bay southwards to Loop Head and takes in the lower reaches of the Shannon Estuary. The beaches provide good fishing for Bass, Ray and Flatfish, while shore fishing from the rocks yields a variety of species.

Several new deep-sea angling boats are now based in the Kilrush area. The deep-sea angling outside Loop Head is believed to be excellent but this area has had very little angling pressure. The sheltered fishing in the estuary has produced superb angling for Tope, Bull Huss, Ray and some Monkfish. Ray and Huss are taken from the shore on a regular basis.

The angling season is from April to October, with some shore fishing extending to December.

■ SHORE ANGLING MARKS (map – page 161)

1. SPANISH POINT: Beach fishing for Bass and Flounder. Spinning for Bass from 'Black Rock' at northern end of beach.

2. DOUGHMORE STRAND: Surf and bottom fishing for Tope, Painted Ray, Bass, Flatfish and Dogfish from southern end of beach. Specimen Painted Ray recorded here. Low and high water best.

3. BALTARD: Bottom fishing, spinning and float fishing for Mackerel, Pollack, Garfish, Wrasse, Spurdog, Conger, Dogfish and Tope. Both sides of headland can be fished. Fishing over foul bottom in very deep water. Specimen Wrasse recorded. This area can be extremely dangerous in rough conditions. Lives have been lost here.

4. KILKEE: Surf fishing from south side of Kilkee Bay for Bass and Flatfish. Spinning from rocks south of town for Pollack and Mackerel.

5. CASTLE POINT: Spinning from rocks for Mackerel and Pollack.

6. CARRIGAHOLT PIER: Bottom fishing from pier for Dabs, Flounder and Dogfish. Spinning and float fishing for Pollack and Wrasse. Night fishing for Conger.

7. MOUTH OF POULNASHERRY BAY: Fishing the Querrin side for Bass and Flatfish at low water and early flood. Occasional Tope, Monkfish and Ray.

8. CAPPAGH PIER (KILRUSH): Bottom fishing into deep water for Dogfish, Bull Huss, Conger and occasional Ray. Small Whiting taken on ragworm.

Cautions: Be careful on rock marks, especially in rough conditions. Extreme caution at Baltard in rough conditions.

■ BAIT (map – page 161)

A. SEAFIELD: Lugworm can be dug near Seafield Pier.
B. RINEVELLA BAY: Some lugworm on beach.
C. CARRIGAHOLT: Soft and peeler crab are plentiful beside the main pier. Lugworm and white rag at inner pier.
D. QUERRIN: Lugworm in estuary near the pier. Crab under weed upstream of pier.
E. KILRUSH GRAVEYARD: Good lugworm digging at end of track below graveyard. Best at low water. Some peeler and soft crab under weed.

■ APPROVED BOATS FOR HIRE

See page 159.

NOTABLE CAPTURES

Species	Weight (lbs)	Location	Bait	Boat/Shore	Date
Cuckoo Wrasse	1.26	Doonbeg	Baited Feathers	B	7/90
Ballan Wrasse	5.9	Doonbeg	Crab	S	9/89
Bass	10 lbs 6 oz	Doughmore	Lugworm	S	1/89
Hake	10 lbs 3 oz	Quilty	Mackerel	B	8/80
Painted Ray	14.06	Doughmore	Mackerel	S	7/79
Tub Gurnard	7.50	Loop Head	Mackerel	B	7/91

COMMON SPECIES

Common Species	Average Size Caught (lbs)
Pollack	6
Coalfish	5
Blue Shark	45
Conger	12
Tope	27
Ling	12
Gurnard	2
Spurdog	6
Greater Spotted Dogfish	11
Thornback Ray	8

TACKLE SHOPS

Jim Robinson, Thomond Shopping Centre, Roxboro, Limerick, (061) 44900

Atlantic Adventures, Frances Street, Kilrush (065) 52133

Michael O'Sullivan, Moore Street, Kilrush

Rosaries Tackle Shop, O'Curry Street, Kilkee

■ CLUBS AND CONTACTS

West Clare SAC, Jacqueline Darcy, 4 Cappagh Drive, Kilrush
Shannon Town SAC, Tom Baracry, Tolka Park, Shannon
Limerick SAC, Dave McCarthy, 91 Gouldavoher Estate,
Limerick (061) 28745

■ COMPETITIONS

A week-long small boat festival takes place in early June each
year based at Kilrush. The Limerick SAC hosts many shore
competitions which are open to visitors throughout the season.
For further details, contact club secretary Dave McCarthy.

■ DESCRIPTION: NORTH CLARE

North Clare enjoys an excellent reputation for its shore
angling, particularly the rock fishing from the numerous
limestone ledges. Species include Ray, Bull Huss and Conger
to double figures. Occasional Porbeagle Shark have also been
landed. This rocky coastline is interspersed with west-facing
storm beaches from which Flatfish, Bass and Ray are taken.

Deep-sea angling is also popular from the two centres,
Ballyvaughan and Liscannor, for Blue and Porbeagle Shark as
well as Tope. There is also excellent general bottom fishing
over a wide range of ground which can produce up to eighteen
different species in a day's fishing. The Aran Islands offer a
base for those anglers on a weekly charter.

The fishing season is from April to October, with some of
the shore angling continuing to December.

This area of the coastline is the only area in Europe from
which numerous Porbeagle Shark up to 145 lbs have been
caught from the shore. Such encounters are always a
possibility during May to October.

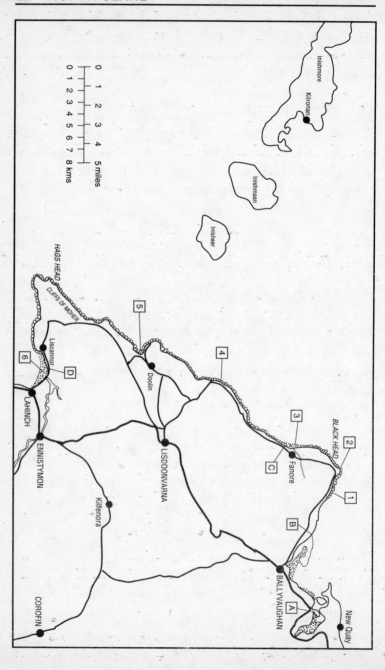

■ SHORE ANGLING MARKS (map – page 166)

1. THE FLATS: Bottom fishing for Ray, Dogfish, Bull Huss, Conger. Spinning for Mackerel and Pollack. Float fishing for Wrasse.

2. BLACK HEAD: Bottom fishing for Dogfish, Conger, Ray, Rockling. Spinning for Mackerel and Pollack. Float fishing for Wrasse. Foul bottom close to shore. Sting Ray have been recorded. Specimen Rockling and Dogfish recorded also.

3. FANORE: Beach fishing for Bass, Flatfish, Dogfish, Bull Huss and Thornback Ray (best at night). Sandeel and Weevers also recorded.

4. BALLYREEN: Bottom fishing for Ray, Conger, Dogfish, Bull Huss and Plaice. Float fishing for Wrasse and Garfish. Spinning for Mackerel and Pollack. Occasional Tope and Porbeagle hooked and landed here. Fishing onto clean ground but foul bottom close to shore.

5. DOOLIN: Beach fishing for Bass, Flatfish and Dogfish. Spinning from rocks at northern end for Bass and Mackerel.

6. MOUTH OF INAGH RIVER: Beach fishing between Liscannor and Lahinch for Bass, Flounder, occasional Plaice and Sea Trout. Moderate surf conditions most productive. Spinning in channel of Inagh River for Bass and Sea Trout. Bottom fishing for Flounder.

■ BAIT (map – page 166)

A. MUCKINISH CASTLE: Good lugworm and small white rag on beach below castle. Some crab around rocky outcrops.

B. RYNN POINT: Lugworm in sandy patches. Crab in rocks and weed at foot of track.

C. FANORE: Sandeel can be dug at low water.

D. LISCANNOR: Lugworm and some white rag on strand below graveyard and to the east of the harbour.

Boat Name	Top Cat
Skipper/Owner	M. Lynch/W. O'Callaghan Rossle, Ennis
Base	Liscannor
Telephone	(065) 21374
Length	11 m (33 ft)
No. of Anglers	8-12
Facilities	Radio, Sounder, Radar, Navigator, Liferaft, Toilet
Daily Charter	£300
Daily Individual	By arrangement
Weekly Charter	By arrangement
Tackle Hire	£5

Boat Name	Lady Christeen	Shark Hunter
Skipper/Owner	M. Lynch/P. Mullen West Country Inn, Ennis, Co. Clare	Kieran O'Driscoll Fisher Street, Doolin Co. Clare
Base	Liscannor	Doolin
Telephone	(065) 21374	(065) 76112 and (088) 575163 Fax (065) 74455
Length	9.8 m (32 ft)	10.3 m (33 ft)
No. of Anglers	Ground–8; Shark–8	Ground–10; Shark–8; Wreck–8
Facilities	Echo, radio, Navigator, Radar	Echo Sounder, Radio, Navigator, Life jackets, Toilet, Washing and Cooking
Daily Charter	£250	£200 (min. daily charge –£160)
Daily Individual	By arrangement	£20
Weekly Charter	£1500	By arrangement
Tackle Hire	£5 per angler	Tackle available

Other boats are available.

NOTABLE CAPTURES

Species	Weight (lbs)	Location	Bait	Boat/Shore	Date
Ballan Wrasse	6.0	Ballyreen	Crab	S	6/90
Ballan Wrasse	5.2	Ballyreen	Crab	S	6/90
Tope	43	New Quay	Mackerel	B	8/91
Ballan Wrasse	5.5	Ballyreen	Crab	S	6/91
Pollack	8.8	Black Head	Rubber Eel	S	7/85
Ling	36.4	Galway Bay	Mackerel	B	8/83
John Dory	6.35	Galway Bay	Pirk	B	8/84

COMMON SPECIES

Common Species	Average Size Caught (lbs)
Blue Shark	45
Porbeagle Shark	70
Tope	26
Ray	10
Ling	10
Pollack (boat)	8
Pollack (shore)	5
Coalfish	4
Conger	15
Whiting	1.5
Bull Huss	9
Ballan Wrasse	3.5

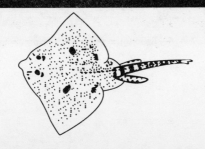

TACKLE SHOPS

M. Tierney, Abbey Street, Ennis
P.J. Keane, Abbey Street, Ennis
Devitts, Main Street, Ennistymon
John MacNamara, Admirals Rest, Fanore
Jim Robinson, Thomond Shopping Centre, Limerick

CLUBS AND CONTACTS

Lisdoonvarna and Fanore SAC, James Linnane,
24 Tullyglass Crescent, Shannon, (061) 62548
John MacNamara, Admirals Rest, Coast Road, Fanore,
Co. Clare, (065) 76105

COMPETITIONS

Two major shore competitions take place each year – the World Rock Championship week in June and the week-long Shore International in August. The comfortable flat rocky ledges are numbered for competitions, offering safe fishing into comparatively deep water.

Galway Bay & Connemara

INTRODUCTION

The expanse of Galway Bay looks like an obvious place for sea angling activity. It's a bit surprising that, up to a couple of years ago, it got very little attention. Local anglers seemed only to have time for game fish. Little was known about the marks and the tourist potential wasn't catered for. But a few dedicated people can make a lot of difference where this kind of apathy is concerned. Those people arrived on the scene in Galway and today things are very different. All this happened at about the time when game fisheries in the county were going through a serious decline. First there was the rod licence dispute which hit particularly hard in this part of the country. Then there was a disastrous decline in Sea Trout stocks leading to a moratorium on angling for the species. This was followed by a less dramatic decline in Salmon runs. Anglers and the angling tourism business needed what the marketing men describe as 'new product' – and they found it in Galway Bay.

Several charter boats with sophisticated electronics set up shop, concentrating on the big game species, Sharks in particular. The initial marketing thrust was towards 'corporate entertainment' – VIPs visiting local factories who probably would have been taken Salmon fishing a few years before. But bookings multiplied from all sorts of clients; the local angling club became more active; 'home tourism' by Irish anglers became a factor, and everything took off.

Finding excellent shore marks for Tope in the north-east corner of the bay certainly helped. But the emphasis is still on boat fishing. The old Porbeagle marks have been rediscovered and have provided excellent sport. Blue Sharks are of top quality and there seem to be plenty of them. Reef and rough ground fishing for bottom species on hard-to-trawl ground around the Aran Islands provides the dessert to the Shark main course.

And one thing Co. Galway has never been short of is a good tourist infrastructure, with plenty of accommodation to suit all pockets and lots of diversion for non-angling family members.

Connemara, certainly south Connemara, also falls into the category of an area of the country with lots of coastline but little sea-angling until very recently. It's a very complex coastline with lots of bays and lagoons. Typically these are shallow, boulder strewn, brackish, full of mariculture cages and hard to fish. The fish species are those that tolerate low salinity, Mullet and Flounders principally and, in the recent past, Sea Trout. A little farther out there are Tope to be caught from dinghies, though these are smaller than the fish at the head of the bay, being mainly male pack-fish in the twenty-five to thirty pound bracket. And farther out again, there is reef and shark fishing over the same ground that the Galway boats fish.

Things get a bit more interesting when you get round as far as Clifden. Here there is a tradition of sea angling with a much longer pedigree than in Galway Bay. There is Shark fishing, general ground fishing and very consistent reef fishing for Pollack, Cod, Ling and Conger. The best of this fishing, weather permitting, is out around High Island.

There is also excellent dinghy fishing in good shelter in the Clifden area with Flats, including some Turbot, Dogs and some of the best Ray fishing in the west of Ireland. It's interesting that some of the Ray marks seem to have declined in the last season or two, and sea anglers are joining with the game anglers in pointing a finger at the ubiquitous Salmon cages as being a possible cause.

Rock species like Wrasse and Pollack from the shore add to the variety of the fishing and the excellent bait beds contrast with something of a bait famine area as far as the rest of the coast covered by this chapter is concerned.

The beaches north of Clifden I don't know well myself. I'm told they are difficult from an angling point of view, being shallow and featureless. The rocky promontories between them are not quite such hard going.

The Killary at the northern boundary of Connemara offers the shore angler deep water with a relatively short cast. The southern shore in particular can be productive, particularly around the youth hostel, for both summer and autumn species. The Sea Trout which used to be a regular part of the sea anglers' catch in the Killary have become very rare over the past couple of seasons.

North of the Killary lies something of a 'Terra Incognita', with miles of rather barren surf beaches which have been known to produce the odd excellent Bass. This bit of coast could be worth exploring, particularly in winter.

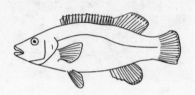

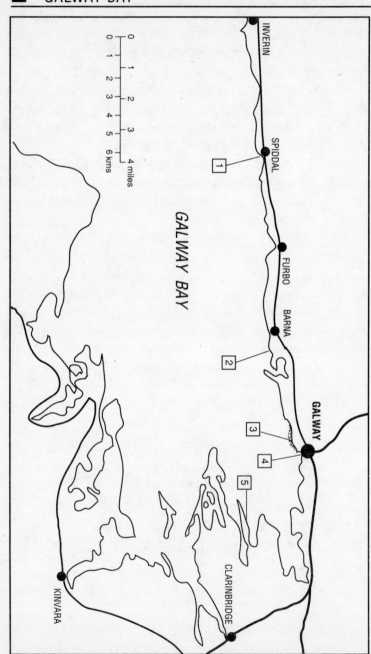

■ DESCRIPTION: GALWAY BAY

In recent years, Galway Bay has re-emerged as one of the top sea angling locations on the west coast. After several years of non-activity, a number of new, fully-equipped charter boats have arrived at Spiddal and the nearby Aran Islands.

Porbeagle Shark are a big attraction during the late summer over the inshore reefs, but consistently good catches of Blue Shark from deep water have given a much needed boost to the area.

Galway City sits astride the famous salmon angling waters of the Corrib system which flows via the Corrib River into the north-eastern corner of the bay. Numerous channels cut through the inner or eastern end of the bay, which is mainly shallow and muddy. As one travels west, however, the bay widens and the seabed becomes sandy, interspersed with several large areas of reef—rich feeding grounds for a wide range of fish species.

The northern shore runs through the holiday villages and towns of Salthill, Barna and Spiddal before turning north into Cashla Bay.

Across the mouth of Galway Bay lie the islands of Inishmore, Inishmaan and Inisheer which make up the Aran Islands, a popular holiday location for thousands of tourists every year, particularly those interested in learning the Irish language which is spoken by virtually all the inhabitants.

As Galway Bay develops again, much will be learnt about the native fish populations, but as a general rule, fishing begins for both boat and shore anglers around mid May and lasts through until the end of September.

■ SHORE ANGLING MARKS (map – page 174)

1. SPIDDAL: Pier fishing at high water over sandy patches for Dab, Plaice and Flounder. Spinning and float fishing from rocks for Pollack, Coalfish and Wrasse.
2. BARNA: Spinning for Bass in the tidal lagoon below the road. Mullet and Flounder are also numerous at times.

3. SALTHILL: Mackerel are plentiful in summer. Night fishing produces Dogfish, Bull Huss, Ray and occasional Bass.
4. GALWAY DOCKS: Conger are fairly plentiful around the quay walls at night, while Mackerel can be taken spinning during the summer. Excellent Mullet fishing is also available from the quay behind the fish plant.
5. RINVILLE/BALLYNACOURTY: Several deep channels run close to the shore at the eastern end of Galway Bay. Recently, these areas have produced excellent shore fishing for Tope, Bull Huss, Dogfish and Ray in May and June.

■ BAIT (map – page 174)

Bait is not very plentiful in this area, although lugworm can usually be dug at low tide on many of the beaches. Fresh Mackerel can be bought from a number of outlets in Galway during the summer months.

■ APPROVED BOATS FOR HIRE

Boat Name	Thresher 1	Aran Striker
Skipper/Owner	Tom Curran Craigmor, Greenhill, Spiddal, Co. Galway	Robert Ellis Aran Deep Sea Angling Centre
Base	Spiddal Pier	Kilronan, Aran Islands
Telephone	(091) 83535	(091) 68903
Length	10 m (33 ft)	12.4 m (40 ft)
No. of Anglers	Shark–10; Bottom–12	Shark –10; Bottom –12
Facilities	Sounder, Radio, Radar, Navigator, Cooking Equip., Toilet, Washup	Sounder, Radio, Radar, Navigator, Toilet, Washup Cooking facilities
Daily Charter	£300 (12 anglers)	£160 min charge
Daily Individual	£30	£20
Weekly Charter	£1500 (6 days)	£960 min. (6 days)
Tackle Hire	Above prices include hire of all tackle.	Shark and bottom outfits £3 daily; £21 weekly

■ NOTABLE CAPTURES

Species	Weight (lbs)	Location	Bait	Boat/Shore	Date
Ballan Wrasse	5.9	Galway Bay	Feathers		10/90

A specimen Tope of 40 lbs was taken by Tony Flannery, Galway Bay SAC, while fishing from the shore near Ballynacourty on Sunday 27 May 1989. The fish was not claimed as a specimen, but was returned alive to the water. Several Blue Shark of over 100 lbs were taken in 1991 but were tagged and returned alive.

■ COMMON SPECIES

Common Species	Average Size Caught(lbs)
Cod	6
Ray	7
Coalfish	5
Tope	28
Whiting	1¼
Mullet	3
Pouting	1
Conger	18
Blue Shark	45
Porbeagle Shark	50
Pollack	5
Dogfish	2

■ TACKLE SHOPS

Galway City Sports (The Great Outdoors), Eglinton Street, Galway

Freeney's, High Street, Galway

Hugh Duffy, 5 Mainguard Street, Galway

T. Naughton and Sons Ltd, 35 Shop Street, Galway

■ CLUBS AND CONTACTS

Cois Fharraige SAC, Fergus Collins, Stripe, Furbo, Co. Galway, (091) 92359
Kilcornan Deep Sea Anglers, Keiran McGrath, Kilcornan
Training Centre, Clarinbridge, Co. Galway, (091) 96106
The Tribes SAC, Michael Naughton, Cushmaigmore, Furbo, Co. Galway, (091) 92416
Galway Bay SAC, Tony Flannery, 18 Rockmount Road, Highfield Park, Galway, (091) 22851

■ COMPETITIONS

Several festivals, shark safaris and shore competitions are staged throughout the year. Further details can be obtained from the club secretaries.

■ DESCRIPTION: ROSSAVEAL TO SLYNE HEAD

Generally the inshore waters and bays are shallow and low in salinity due to the large numbers of rivers and streams entering the sea here. The coastline is very indented and rugged and the shoreline is heavily covered with bladderwrack. Due to these factors, the fish population is restricted to those species with a tolerance for the conditions. The deeper, offshore waters offer good opportunities for reef and clean ground fishing.

Sea angling is totally under-developed in this area and has only emerged as a serious tourist attraction in the last number of years. Due to the lack of angling pressure, there is no history of specimen or record fish. This is set to change, however, with the arrival of several new angling charter craft.

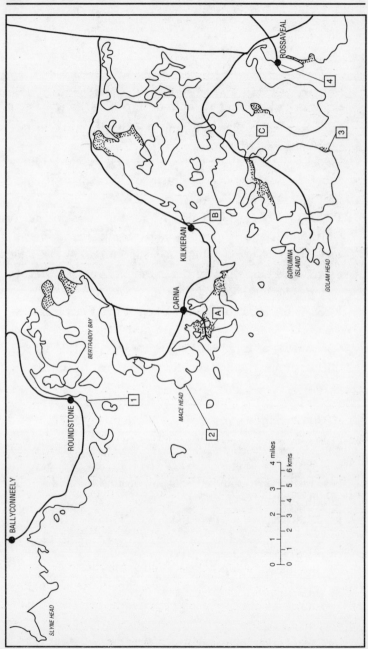

GALWAY BAY & CONNEMARA

ROSSAVEAL

KILKIERAN

CARNA

GORUMNA ISLAND

GOLAM HEAD

BERTRABOY BAY

MACE HEAD

ROUNDSTONE

BALLYCONNEELY

SLYNE HEAD

0 1 2 3 4 miles
0 1 2 3 4 5 6 kms

179

Shore fishing is increasing in popularity and the local angling club at Carna organises several shore events in the season. Generally, fishing is best from May to September.

■ SHORE ANGLING MARKS (map – page 179)

1. GORTEEN BAY: About a mile south-west of Roundstone, there is rock fishing at the mouth of Bertraboy Bay for Pollack, Wrasse and Dogfish. Occasional Ray are also a possibility over sand.

2. MACE HEAD: Fishing close to the rock provides Wrasse and Pollack, while distance casters will reach sand where Ray, Bull Huss and Dogfish can be taken.

3. TRAWBAUN HARBOUR: On the south-east corner of Gorumna Island is a small sandy creek surrounded by rock. From the quay, fishing over sand produces Flounder, Plaice and Dabs. Spinning from the rocky outcrops accounts for Pollack and Coalfish.

4. ROSSAVEAL: Conger can be taken at night just inside the pier head. Bottom fishing over mud will produce Flounder. Vast shoals of large Mullet are resident in the harbour during summer, but pre-baiting is required to entice them to feed.

■ BAIT (map – page 179)

A. MWEENISH BAY: Lugworm and some white ragworm can be dug on the beach, while crab can be gathered at the base of the surrounding rocks and around the rocks in the middle of the bay.

B. KILKIERAN: Just north of the village, lugworm can be dug on the shore just below the road.

C. LETTERMORE AND GORUMNA: Crab are plentiful in the weed around both islands, while lugworm can be dug in muddy patches.

APPROVED BOATS FOR HIRE

Boat Name	Reuben Bulmar II	Gina Maria
Skipper/Owner	Pat Conneely Roundstone, Co. Galway	Pat Conneely Roundstone, Co. Galway
Base	Roundstone Pier	Roundstone Pier
Telephone	(095) 35854	(095) 35854
Length	9.8 m (32 ft)	15.2 m (50 ft)
No. of Anglers	Shark–9; Bottom–9	Shark–12; Bottom–12
Facilities	Sounder, Radio, Navigator, Toilet, Washup, Cooking equipment	Sounder, Radio, Navigator, Radar, Toilet Washup, Cooking facilities
Daily Charter	£90	£140
Daily Individual	£15	£15
Weekly Charter	£540 (6 days)	£840 (6 days)
Tackle Hire	£3	Shark and bottom outfits – £3 daily

NOTABLE CAPTURES

Species	Weight (lbs)	Location	Bait	Boat/Shore	Date
Pollack	12.68	Roundstone	Rubber Eel	B	9/91
Blue Shark	102.00	Slyne Head	Mackerel	B	8/91

COMMON SPECIES

Common Species	Average Size Caught (lbs)
Ray	8
Dogfish	2
Bull Huss	10
Conger	9
Pollack	4
Coalfish	2
Dab	.75
Wrasse	3

■ TACKLE SHOPS

The nearest tackle shop is in Clifden.

■ CLUBS AND CONTACTS

Carna SAA: Duncan Brown, Mweenish, Carna, Co. Galway, (095) 32296 (home), (095) 32201 (work)

■ CLIFDEN

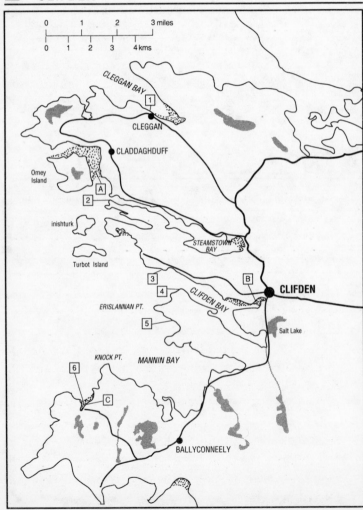

■ DESCRIPTION: CLIFDEN

Set in the heart of Connemara, Clifden has been established as a sea angling centre for some twenty years.

The variety of sea fishing on offer varies from shore fishing for Ray from a number of sheltered deep water locations, to offshore boat fishing over reefs around many of the islands for Pollack and Cod. Shark fishing too has always been popular in the summer months.

The area boasts a well-equipped charter fleet and experienced skippers and in recent years, has attracted increasingly large numbers of continental visitors.

The season for both boat and shore angling extends from May to September, but good boat fishing can be experienced into November, weather permitting.

■ SHORE ANGLING MARKS (map – page 182)

1. CLEGGAN PIER: Conger (particularly on night tides) and Flounder. Occasionally Mullet congregate in the bay.
2. COOLACLOY: Spinning for Pollack, Coalfish and Mackerel (in season). Float fishing for Wrasse and bottom fishing for Conger and Dogfish.
3. SLOPERS CLIFF AND BELEEK: Bottom fishing over sand for Dabs, Dogfish and Ray. Spinning for Pollack and Mackerel (in season). Float fishing for Coalfish and Wrasse. Bottom fishing over foul ground for Conger.
4. WHITE LADY: Bottom fishing over sand for Ray, Dogfish, Plaice and Dabs. Spinning for Pollack and Mackerel in season. Float fishing for Wrasse.
5. BALLINAGA AND CANDOOLIN: Bottom fishing over mixed ground for Ray, Dabs, Plaice, Founder, small Turbot and Dogfish. Float fishing in rocky areas for Wrasse.
6. DOONLOUGHAN: Bottom fishing in sandy patches for Flounder, small Turbot, Plaice and occasional Ray and Dogfish at night.

Special features:

Most shore venues are signposted.

Cautions: Care should be taken on all rock marks, particularly Slopers Cliff and The White Lady.

■ BAIT

A. OMEY ISLAND: Lugworm on banks between island and mainland. Occasional clam on south-eastern side of sand bar.

B. CLIFDEN HARBOUR: Digging on banks of channel for sandeel, razor fish and some white ragworm. Large lugworm below boat moorings.

C. DOONLOUGHAN: Lugworm in sandy patches.

■ APPROVED BOATS FOR HIRE

Boat Name	Lagosta	Wild Rover	Celtic Queen	Lady Maureen
Skipper/Owner	John Brittain Blue Water Fishing, Errislannin, Clifden	John Ryan Dun Aengus, Sky Road, Clifden	John Ryan Dun Aengus, Sky Road Clifden	Jan Smits Coolacloy, Clifden
Base	Clifden Quay	Clifden Quay	Clifden Quay	Clifden Quay
Telephone	(095) 21073	(095) 21069	(095) 21069	(095) 21787
Length	9.4 m (31 ft)	10 m (33 ft)	16.5 m (54 ft)	10 m (33 ft)
No. of Anglers	Shark–6; Bottom–12	Shark–8; Bottom–10	Shark–8; Bottom –12	Shark 6–8; Bottom –12
Facilities	Sounder, Radio, Navigator, Liferaft, Toilet, Washup	Sounder, Radio, Navigator, Toilet, Washup Cooking	Sounder, Radio, Radar, Navigator, Toilet, Washup, Cooking	Sounder, Radio, Navigator, Toilet, Washup, Cooking
Daily Charter	£100	£160	£300 (12 pers.) (min. charge £160)	£160 (12 pers.) (min. charge £60)
Daily Individual	£22	£20	£30	£900
Weekly Charter	£600 (6 days)	£1000–5 days	By arrangement	By arrangement
Tackle Hire	Shark and bottom outfits – £5 daily	Shark and bottom outfits – £5 daily; £30 weekly	Shark and bottom outfits – £5 daily; £30 weekly	Shark and bottom outfits – £5 daily; £20 weekly

NOTABLE CAPTURES

Species	Weight (lbs)	Location	Bait	Boat/Shore	Date
Ballan Wrasse	5.41	Clifden	Mackerel	B	10/88
Freshwater Eel	4.25	Aughrusbeg	Sprat	S	6/89
Garfish	2.85	Clifden	Mackerel	B	10/90
Pollack	13.20	Clifden	Mackerel	B	9/90
Blue Shark	120.00	Clifden	Mackerel	B	9/90
L. S. Dogfish	3.50	Clifden	Mackerel	B	6/91
Plaice	4.25	Clifden	Mackerel	B	6/91
Pollack	13.12	Clifden	Sandeel	B	6/91

COMMON SPECIES

Common Species	Average Size Caught (lbs)
Cod	7
Ray	8
Pollack	7
Coalfish	4
Gurnard	2
Conger	12
Whiting	1
Pouting	1
Dogfish	2
Turbot	6
Wrasse	3

TACKLE SHOP

Paddy Pryce, Main Street, Clifden

CLUBS AND CONTACTS

Paddy Pryce, Main Street, Clifden (a good source of
information on local fishing)
There is no sea angling club in Clifden.

COMPETITIONS

No competitions are staged in Clifden.

Westport & Achill Island

INTRODUCTION

We are now getting into an area which could justifiably call itself the capital of sea angling in the west. Westport is particularly famous for its annual June Sea Angling Festival, which has been going for over thirty years non-stop and is the oldest in this country, and possibly in the world.

The remarkable topography of Clew Bay is one of the reasons for all this fame. There are supposed to be 365 islands in its shallow waters, and these islands provide shelter whatever the weather. Add to this specimens of large and exotic fish like Skate and Monk and you have a formula that can't fail.

In recent years, the best of the fishing has been in deeper water out around Clare Island in the mouth of the bay; modern, fast charter boats have been taking the place of the old half-deckers. One of the reasons for the change was that in the old days when I first fished Clew Bay, sea angling conservation had never been heard of and, after a major competition, literally tons of inedible fish were left rotting in the harbour.

The stocks couldn't take this sort of pressure and they declined, so boats had to go farther and farther to get fish.

Things are very different today, and Clew Bay is in the forefront of the catch-and-release movement. The stocks are coming back in the shallow water. In fact, there are marks today where you can take Tope and occasional Monks from the shore, along with more conventional Ray, Dogs and Huss.

One of the features of the bay is island shore fishing. A boat deposits you on one of those islands in the morning. You fish away all day and it picks you up in the evening. Unusual and very enjoyable particularly if, like me, you have a thing about islands.

Mallaranny Pier offers yet another type of fishing from the shore, with Wrasse, Conger, Pollack and a surprising number of rare vagrants from the Gulf Stream like Trigger Fish. Newport offers superb fishing for large Mullet.

But to get back to the charter boat fishing which is the main characteristic of the sport out of both Westport and Newport. Offshore marks like Deacey's Rock and Inisturk Island offer a wealth of ground, much of it unexplored. The angling is mainly on reefs which the commercial men find hard to exploit and small patches of sandy ground between the reefs. Good Blue Shark fishing has been developed in the same area in recent years.

One of the things that always fascinates me about Clew Bay is that it was the headquarters, in Elizabethan times, of the great warrior queen, Granuaile, who was definitely an early feminist. Some of her influence seems to have lingered on to this day because sea angling, something of a macho male sport in most parts of the world, is far from that in this part of Mayo. Clew Bay Ladies SAC is the only women's sea angling club in the country. No less than four women anglers from the bay have, over the years, made it in open competition, on to the Irish International Team, a record surely without parallel anywhere in the world.

These fine anglers are Mary Gavin-Hughes, who is also an excellent charter boat skipper, Bella Moran, Hilda Clinton and Mairin Lambert. I have fished with some of them – an experience which taught me a lot, both about angling and about sexual stereotyping.

Achill Island also has a special place in the history of sea angling. A lot of pioneering work on the development of cold water big game fishing was carried on here in the early decades of the century. And to this day, Achill holds our two Shark records, and masses of specimen claims.

Dr O Donel-Brown took his record 365 lbs Porbeagle off Achill in 1932 and J. McMonagle caught his record 206 lbs Blue in 1959. And even if these records stand for all time, it may not be the end of the story. Several Threshers and at least one definite Mako have been seen in the area in recent years. These are much bigger sharks than Porbeagles or Blues and there is no rod and line record for them in Irish waters... yet.

With all this history and all this potential, it seems a little strange that there is no full-time professional charter boat on Achill today. Most of the angling interest centres on shore fishing, and in particular on beautiful Keem Strand where, beside the ruined remains of an old commercial Basking Shark fishery, you can cast out into water of pellucid cleanness and catch a great variety of flats and round fish.

■ DESCRIPTION: WESTPORT

Westport is famous for its international sea angling festival, the first in Ireland and one of the longest running events of its kind in Europe. The event takes place every year in late June. The town has also been the scene of many other major sea angling events, culminating in the CIPS World Boat Angling Championships in 1991.

Clew Bay offers fishing in virtually any weather conditions among the 365 islands.

In recent years, the most exciting fishing has been found in the deeper water around Clare Island. This fishing has been opened up due to the arrival of fast purpose-built sea-angling charter boats, of which several now operate successfully.

Boats are generally available from April, with the fishing season lasting through to the end of September. In calm conditions, boats have ventured forth as late as December with good results. Shore angling has increased in popularity in recent years. Fishing to date has generally been confined to the summer months of June, July and August. Common Skate and Monkfisk are regularly caught but always returned alive.

■ SHORE ANGLING MARKS (map – page 190)

1. CORRAUN PENINSULA: Spinning from rocks at various stations for Pollack, Mackerel, Coalfish and occasional Garfish. Bottom fishing over mixed ground for Dogfish, Ray, Conger and occasional Flounder and Plaice. Float fishing for Wrasse.
2. MALLARANNY: Beach fishing for Dogfish, small Turbot, Ray, Flounder, Dab and occasional Bass. Specimen Bass recorded. Pier fishing for Ray, Pollack, Coalfish, Wrasse.
3. BERTRA STRAND: Spinning close to stony reef in middle of western-facing beach for Mackerel, occasional Bass and Sea Trout. Specimen Bass recorded. Beach fishing for

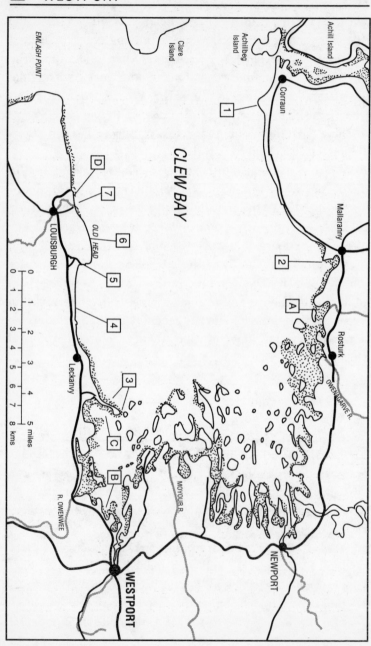

Flounder. Spinning from the point on the first two hours of the flood for Mackerel, Pollack, occasional Bass and Sea Trout. Bottom fishing for Dogfish, Bull Huss and occasional Tope. In the deep slack water pool, east of Bertra Island, Ray and Monkfish may also be encountered by distance casters.

4. KILSALLAGH: Spinning from rocks below old schoolhouse at high water for Pollack and Mackerel in season. Float fishing close to the rock for Wrasse and Coalfish. Casting over sand for Dab, Dogfish and Ray.

5. OLD HEAD PIER: Spinning in summer for Mackerel and small Pollack. Bottom fishing for Dogfish, Flounder, Dab and occasional Ray and Bass. Night tides best. This pier is tidal.

6. OLD HEAD: Spinning from various rock platforms for Pollack, Coalfish and occasional Sea Trout, Mackerel and Garfish in season. Float fishing for Wrasse. Bottom fishing over sandy patches for Plaice, Dab, Gurnard, Pouting, Dogfish, Bull Huss and occasional Ray and Conger.

7. CARROWMORE STRAND: Surf fishing for Flounder, Dab, occasional Sea Trout and Bass. Mullet have also been taken on small fish baits near river mouth. First two hours of flood tide and high water most productive.

■ BAIT (map – page 190)

A. ROSSMURREVAGH: Lugworm and clam on western bank of Bunnahowna River.

B. ROSBEG: Lugworm and clam (especially opposite quay). Razorfish at low water springs.

C. MURRISK: Lugworm (mainly small but in vast numbers). Occasional clam.

D. CARROWMORE STRAND: Sandeel can be dug on low water springs. Occasional razorfish and white ragworm.

■ APPROVED BOATS FOR HIRE

Boat Name	Corulan	Lady Helen	Shamrock
Skipper/Owner	Francis Clarke The Mews, Rosbeg, Westport, Co. Mayo	Reg Roynan Rosmoney, Westport, Co. Mayo	Mary Gavin-Hughes Clynish View, Darradda, Newport
Base	Westport Quay	Westport Quay	Roigh Pier
Telephone	(098) 25481	(098) 26514	(098) 41562
Length	10 m (33 ft)	11 m (36 ft)	8 m (26 ft)
No. of Anglers	Shark–8; Ground–10	Shark–6; Ground–8	Ground–8
Facilities	Sounder, Radio, Radar, Navigator, Toilet, Washup, Cooking facilities	Sounder, Radio, Navigator, Toilet, Washup, Cooking facilities	Radio, Sounder Toilet, Washup
Daily Charter	£120	£120	£112
Daily Individual	£15	£15	£14
Weekly Charter	£720 (6 days)	£720 (6 days)	By arrangement
Tackle Hire	Bottom outfit– £3 daily	Shark and Bottom outfits – £2 daily, £14 weekly	Bottom outfit £5 daily

A large number of other boats are available at weekends or for competitions.

■ NOTABLE CAPTURES

Species	Weight (lbs)	Location	Bait	Boat/Shore	Date
Cod	28.25	Westport	Baited feathers	B	7/86
L.S. Dogfish	4.25	Clare Island	Mackerel	B	8/86
Grey Gurnard	1.63	Westport	Mackerel	B	9/86
Red Gurnard	2.25	Clew Bay	Mackerel	B	8/90
Homelyn Ray	5.50	Clew Bay	Mackerel	B	6/90
Tub Gurnard	5.0	Clew Bay	Mackerel	B	8/91
Blue Shark	102.0	Clew Bay	Mackerel	B	8/91
Grey Mullet	6.20	L. Furnace	Bread	S	8/91

■ IRISH RECORD

White Skate   105 lbs   7/8/1966

COMMON SPECIES

Common Species	Average Size Caught (lbs)
Pollack	5
Coalfish	6.5
Lesser Spotted Dogfish	2
Greater Spotted Dogfish	8
Ray	6
Common Skate	80
Cod	6.5
Ling	8
Gurnard	2
Monkfish	30
Whiting	1

TACKLE SHOPS

Tackle Box, Angling Centre, The Quay, Westport, (098) 25283

Hewetsons, Bridge Street, Westport

Paddy Ward, Shop Street, Westport

Marine Supplies (Hugh O'Donnell), Shop Street, Westport, (098) 25182

CLUBS AND CONTACTS

Allergan SAC, Nicky Lambert, Altamont Street, Westport, (098) 25704

Clew Bay Ladies SAC, Mairin Lambert, Altamont Street, Westport, (098) 25704

Newport SAC, Alec Latto, 5 Quay Road, Westport, (098) 26514

Westport Boat Club, John Foy, Reek View, Westport, Co. Mayo, (098) 25283 (Angling Centre)

Westport SAC, Francis Clarke, The Mews, Rosbeg, Westport, (098) 25481

COMPETITIONS

Clew Bay is the scene of more boat angling competitions per year than any other venue in the country. On almost any weekend through the year, events are staged there, with the two best attended being the National Interfirm Championship and International Festival, both in June.

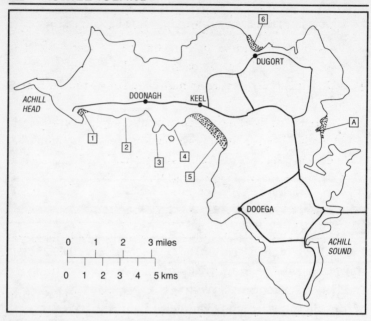

DESCRIPTION: ACHILL ISLAND

Achill is the largest island off the Irish coast and is connected by a road bridge to the mainland at Achill Sound. The offshore waters offer a wealth of first-class deep sea angling. Both the Irish Porbeagle (365 lbs) and Blue Shark (206 lbs) records are held here.

Shore angling is becoming increasingly popular on the island, with several first-class marks being discovered in the last few years.

SHORE ANGLING MARKS (map – page 194)

1. KEEM STRAND: Beach fishing for Turbot, Dab, Flounder, Plaice, Dogfish and occasional Sole. Distance casting produces Ray and Codling.
2. CARRICKMORE: Rock fishing for Coalfish, Pollack, Wrasse, Conger and Dogfish. Very foul ground and deep water.

3. ALENNAUN MOR: Rock fishing into deep water over foul ground for Conger, Pollack, Coalfish and Wrasse. Sandy patches hold Dogfish, Bull Huss, Dab and occasional Ray. 20 minute walk from car park but can be worth the long hike. Should only be approached in calm conditions.

4. PURTEEN: Pier fishing at high water for Mullet, Conger and Wrasse.

5. KEEL: Beach fishing (particularly at night) for Turbot, Dab, Flounder, Dogfish and occasional Ray, Sea Trout and Bass.

6. DUGORT: Pier and rock fishing for Coalfish, Pollack, Conger, Flounder, Dogfish and Ray.

■ BAIT (map – page 194)

A. BUNNACURRY: Soft and peeler crab can be gathered at low water (in season). Mussel can be gathered on low rocks while lugworm can be dug on mudflats.
Note: Mackerel can usually be obtained (in season) from the boatmen at Purteen Harbour.

■ APPROVED BOATS FOR HIRE

There are no registered charter craft in the area, but local fishermen can usually be persuaded to take out anglers at weekends.

■ NOTABLE CAPTURES

Species	Weight (lbs)	Location	Bait	Boat/Shore	Date
Coalfish	17.30	off Achill	Redgill	B	8/87
Red Gurnard	2.3	off Achill	Mackerel	B	8/88
Tub Gurnard	6.21	off Achill	Baited feathers	B	8/89
Blue Shark	112.5	off Achill	Mackerel	B	9/89
L.S. Dogfish	3.83	off Achill	Mackerel strip	B	8/90
Megrim	2.33	off Achill	Mackerel	B	8/90
Pollack	12.30	off Achill	Baited feathers	B	7/90

■ IRISH RECORDS

Species	Weight (lbs)	Location	Bait	Boat/Shore	Date
Tub Gurnard	12.24	Bullsmouth	Mackerel	B	8/73
Porbeagle Shark	365	Keem Bay	Mackerel	B	1932
Blue Shark	206	Achill Head	Mackerel	B	10/59

■ COMMON SPECIES

Common Species	Average Size Caught (lbs)
Cod	7
Ray	8
Coalfish	7
Gurnard	2
Conger	13
Whiting	1.5
Pouting	1
Dogfish	2.5
Pollack	6

■ TACKLE SHOP

Stand Sports Shop, Keel PO, Keel, (098) 43125

■ CLUBS AND CONTACTS

Achill Junior SAC, Julie Hassett, 'Cuan na Gaoithe',
Pollagh, Keel, Achill (098) 43265
Achill SAC, John O'Shea, Dooagh, Achill, (098) 43112
Currane SAC, Shiela Joyce, Bunanioo, Currane PO, Westport,
(098) 45421
Mallaranny SAC, Caroline Ginnelly, Rossork, Westport,
(098) 36152
Saula SAC, Rev. Fr Pat. Donnellan, The Presbytery,
Achill Sound, (098) 45109

■ COMPETITIONS

Several major festivals, shark safaris and shore competitions
are staged annually. Further details from club secretaries.

Belmullet & Killala Bay

Belmullet is a wonderful angling centre, certainly under-used. It is, it must be admitted, a long way from anywhere else. It is the capital of the Barony of Erris which is a wonderful wilderness of lowland blanket bog and mountain in one of the least spoilt areas of the whole country.

The town is on a little isthmus dividing two great bays of fairly shallow and well sheltered water. On the southernmost of these bays, Blacksod, a sea angling club was formed in the mid sixties. The club was the brain child of a local priest and unashamedly a tourist development tool. Nobody, in fact, knew anything about the angling potential.

The Inland Fisheries Trust, which was the precursor of the Central Fisheries Board, set about helping the locals rectify this and one of the things Des Brennan and Kevin Linnane did was to invite over some of the most famous British sea angling writers of the day, such as Clive Gammon.

They had good weather the first day and they steamed out of the bay, beyond the Inishkea Islands to the Black Rock Light. Coming back in the evening they had over half a ton of fish of eight to ten species, including fine Cod, and several specimen Pollack and Bream.

197

The amazing potential of the area was underlined the next day when a Force Ten gale blew up, as so often happens off this Atlantic coast. The Black Rock Light was out of the question but Belmullet gives access to those two shallow sheltered bays. Five rods went out in a twenty-six foot double-ender into the northern bay, Broadhaven. This time they had three-quarters of a ton of fish in twelve feet of water! They included Tope, Ray, Gurnard and *boxes* of Turbot!

Of course, things have quietened down a little bit since those heady pioneering days of a quarter of a century ago. Most of the Turbot have been cleaned out by commercial fishermen. But other species have been discovered and many anglers, mostly from English and North of Ireland clubs, have made annual pilgrimages to this part of west Mayo to add to the book of angling knowledge opened by Des Brennan, Kevin Linnane, Hugh Stoker and Clive Gammon in 1966.

Exciting shallow water marks for Monkfish have been discovered in the inner shelter of Blacksod and altogether over thirty species have been recorded, including former Irish record Bull Huss and Turbot and the present records for Red Gurnard and Halibut, as well as some unusual fish like Megrim to attract the specimen hunter wanting to add another species to his list.

The original fishing concentrated heavily on charter boat operators. They're still there and they can still deliver the fish. But in recent years there has been a growing emphasis on self-drive dinghies in the sheltered waters of the two great bays and in exploring the exciting potential of the shore angling.

North of Belmullet the Erris Race off Erris Head has always been famous for large Coalies and Haddock. The Haddock disappeared almost completely, probably as a result of commercial pressure, but there are some signs of a come-back. This is another area where interest in shore angling has been growing in recent years.

Round the next corner there's a set of impressive sea stacks called the Stags. I'm always amazed by the sheep grazing on them. It's said that when they are fattened the only way to remove them is with a rifle and a boat; I've never solved the mystery of how they get them on there in the first place!

Killala Bay has been popular with tourists, angling and otherwise, for some years now. It has two harbours, each with its own club. The fact that the John Dory record is held here is probably a reminder that this bit of Mayo is the nearest point in the country to the edge of the continental shelf. But in the records of the Specimen Fish Committee, Killala is famous for Hake. In 1978 eighteen Hake over the specimen weight of 10 lbs were claimed. Seventeen of them were caught by anglers out of Enniscrone on the Sligo side of the bay and all seventeen were caught on two days! On 24 July a party of German anglers met the shoal of monsters and had fish up to 22 lbs 8 oz. The jumbo shoal was encountered again by a boat of Dutchmen on 4 August and that made up the total of seventeen huge fish. The shoal was never seen again and Hake are a relatively uncommon species in the area today.

Shore fishing is also popular in the Killala area and one of the bonuses is that Sea Trout, a fish that's declining rapidly over much of the western sea-board, are still plentiful here and often taken by shore-anglers. In fact there is a regular angling fishery specifically for Sea Trout in the Moy estuary using drift-lined Sand Eel.

This is the obvious place to remind all-round anglers that this part of the country provides some of the best conventional game-fishing in Ireland. There are excellent Salmon, Sea Trout and Brown Trout in north-west Mayo. You can't expect to walk in off the street and get on to the very best of it, like the famous Ridge Pool on the Moy in Ballina, but there's lots of Salmon and Sea Trout water freely available at low cost or even free to anyone holding a licence, and you don't even need a licence to fish for the excellent Brown Trout on Loughs Conn and Cullen.

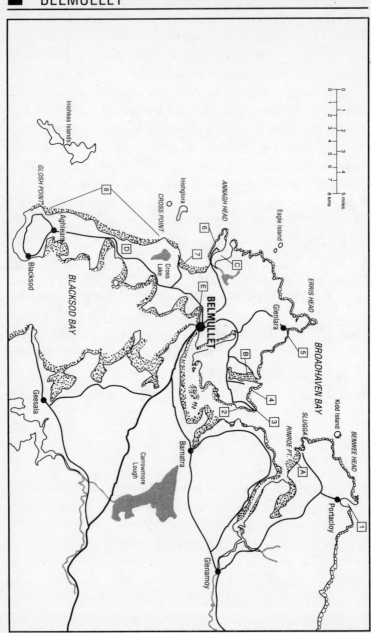

DESCRIPTION: BELMULLET

Belmullet boasts some of the finest boat fishing in Ireland, with possibly the widest variety of fish in the country. The two bays of Broadhaven in the north and Blacksod in the south offer sea fishing in virtually all weather conditions.

Some of the better-known offshore marks are: The Stags at Porturlin, Erris Race on Broadhaven, Eagle Island at Frenchport and Black Rock off Blacksod. Shore fishing is excellent during the summer months, but little is known about winter fishing.

SHORE ANGLING MARKS (map – page 200)

1. PORTACLOY: Bottom fishing from inner pier for Ray, Turbot, Flounder, Dogfish, Plaice, Dab and Gurnard. Float fishing for Wrasse. Spinning from both piers at high water for Mackerel, Coalfish and Pollack.

2. BALLYGLASS PIER: Bottom fishing for Ray, Turbot, Flounder, Conger, Plaice, Dogfish and occasional Codling. Float fishing and spinning for Coalfish and Pollack. Specimen Mullet recorded.

3. BALLYGLASS POINT: Spinning on either side of ravine for Mackerel, Pollack and small Coalfish. Bottom fishing for Dogfish and Conger. Float fishing for Wrasse.

4. POLLACOPPAL: Beach fishing for Ray, Flounder, Dab and small Turbot. Night tides best.

5. GLENLARA: Bottom fishing from rock platform for Conger, Dogfish and Rockling. Float fishing for Wrasse and spinning for Pollack and Coalfish.

6. ANNAGH HEAD: Spinning for Pollack, Coalfish and Mackerel. Float fishing for Wrasse. Bottom fishing for Dogfish and Conger. Very foul ground.
   Caution: This area is very dangerous in heavy swells and should not be approached in these conditions.

7. CROSS STRAND: Bottom fishing in surf for Flounder, Sea Trout, Dogfish and small Turbot. Occasional Ray and Bull Huss in calm conditions at night.

8. CROSS POINT TO GLOSH TOWER: Beach fishing all along here, especially near rocky outcrops for Flounder, Dab, Dogfish, small Turbot and occasional Ray, Sea Trout and Bass. Specimen Sea Trout recorded.

■ BAIT (map – page 200)

A. RINROE: Lugworm and crab east of pier. Sandeel in channel.
B. BLIND HARBOUR: Lugworm south of slipway.
C. FRENCHPORT: Lugworm east of pier. Crab in weed margins.
D. ELLY BAY: Lugworm immediately below car park.
E. BELMULLET: Lugworm and clam on beach behind pumphouse and opposite creamery west of town. Crab around rocks on Shore Road.

■ APPROVED BOATS FOR HIRE

Boat Name	Arran More	Girl Deborah
Skipper/Owner	Pauraic Sheeran Carne, Belmullet	Tom Nallon Belmullet
Base	Belmullet	Ballyglass
Telephone	(097) 81105	(097) 81424
Length	11.5 m (38 ft)	11.5 m (38 ft)
No. of Anglers	10 Bottom fishing	8-10 Bottom fishing
Facilities	Radio, Sounder, Radar, Toilet, Cooking facilities	Radio, Sounder Navigator, Toilet, Cooking facilities
Daily Charter	£100 (min. £80)	£100 (min. £80)
Daily Individual	£15	£15
Weekly Charter	£700	£700
Tackle Hire	Bottom outfit £2.50	Bottom outfit £2.50

Boat Name	Girl Emer	Orla Marie
Skipper/Owner	V. Sweeney Blacksod, Ballina	Michael Lavelle Aughleam, Blacksod, Ballina
Base	Blacksod Quay	Blacksod Quay
Telephone	(097) 85662 or (097) 85774	(097) 85669
Length	9.1 m (30 ft)	8.9 m (29 ft)
No. of Anglers	Shark–4; Ground–6	Shark–8; Bottom–8
Facilities	Echo Sounder	Radio, Sounder, Radar, Navigator, Toilet, Washup, Cooking Equip.
Daily Charter	£100	£100 (£80 min.)
Daily Individual	£15	£15
Weekly Charter	£600	£600
Tackle Hire	£3.00 daily	Shark outfit – £5 daily, £20 weekly; Bottom outfit – £3 daily, £12 weekly

Other boats are also available at weekends and for competitions.

■ NOTABLE CAPTURES

Species	Weight (lbs)	Location	Bait	Boat/Shore	Date
Ballan Wrasse	4.76	Broadhaven	Feathers	B	9/87
Blonde Ray	25.50	Erris Head	Mackerel	B	8/90
Coalfish	15	Broadhaven	Spoon	B	8/87
Dab	1.72	Blacksod	Rag/Mackerel	B	7/86
Grey Gurnard	2.24	Broadhaven	Mackerel	B	7/91
Megrim	2.40	Erris Head	Mackerel Strip	B	8/86
Red Gurnard	2.21	Broadhaven	Baited Spoon	B	8/86
Torsk	6.28	Broadhaven	Pirk	B	8/88
Tub Gurnard	6.04	Broadhaven	Mackerel	B	8/90
Cuckoo Wrasse	1.45	Broadhaven	Mackerel	B	8/91

IRISH RECORDS

Species	Weight (lbs)	Location	Bait	Boat/Shore	Date
Red Gurnard	3.61	Broadhaven	Mackerel	B	7/68
Halibut	156	'Stags'	Baited Feathers	B	7/72

COMMON SPECIES

Common Species	Average Size Caught (lbs)
Cod	4
Whiting	1.5
Pollack	7
Coalfish	7
Ray	8
Monkfish	30
Tope	25
Turbot	9
Ling	8
Conger	13

TACKLE SHOPS

Coyle's, American Street, Belmullet
Erris Co-op, Chapel Street, Belmullet

CLUBS AND CONTACTS

Belmullet SAC: Gerry Murphy, Church Road, Belmullet, (097) 81195
Buddy Valkenburg, The Square, Belmullet, (097) 81076

COMPETITIONS

Belmullet SAC organises several major tournaments every year. The top event is the annual festival which normally takes place in mid August.

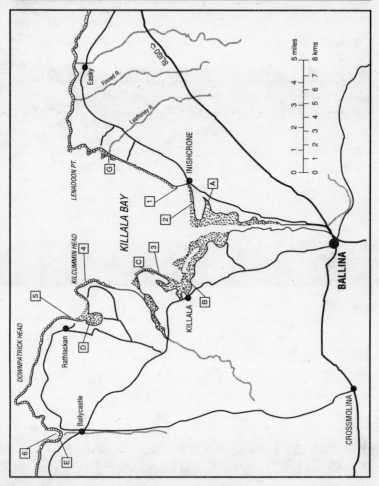

■ **DESCRIPTION: KILLALA BAY**

Killala Bay has an international reputation for its sea angling festivals. Several major events are organised each year and attract many visitors.

A wide range of species is available to boat anglers, including Ray, Dogfish, Turbot, Megrim and Dabs over sand, to Conger, Ling, Pollack and Coalfish from the reef marks. Codling are very prolific. Shore angling is becoming increasingly popular and several locations offer excellent sport. Until recently there was no approved charter boat on the bay, but in 1991 a new full time boat arrived to cater for the large numbers of annual visitors.

■ SHORE ANGLING MARKS (map – page 205)

1. INISHCRONE PIER: Bottom fishing for Conger, Dogfish and occasional Ray and Flatfish. Spinning for small Pollack and Mackerel. High tide best.
2. INISHCRONE STRAND: Beach fishing for Flounder, Dab, Dogfish and occasional Bass (in surf conditions), Ray (in calm weather) and Sea Trout.
3. SCURMORE: Spinning and bottom fishing for Sea Trout and bottom fishing for Flounder.
4. KILCUMMIN AND THE FLAGS: Rock fishing for Pollack, Coalfish, Wrasse and occasional Conger.
5. LACKAN PIER: Spinning for Pollack, Mackerel and Coalfish. Float fishing for Wrasse. Bottom fishing for Flounder in sandy patches and Conger over rough ground. Beach fishing from strand for Flounder, Sea Trout, Turbot, Dab, Dogfish, Coalfish and occasional Ray.
6. BALLYCASTLE: Beach fishing for Flounder, Dogfish, Coalfish and Codling. Night tides with low water and first two hours of flood best.

■ BAIT (map – page 205)

A. MOY ESTUARY (EAST SIDE): Lugworm and clam.
B. STANDING STONE: Lugworm and clam on banks of channel. Crab in weed around rocky margins.
C. KILLALA CHANNEL: Lugworm (mainly small but in vast numbers) on channel bank. Crab among boulders.
D. LACKAN ESTUARY: Sandeel on channel banks. Lugworm in patches.
E. BALLYCASTLE STRAND: Lugworm below carpark and crab around base of reef.

Frozen bait can be purchased from J. Walkin, Tone Street, Ballina.

■ APPROVED BOAT FOR HIRE

Boat Name	Patrick J
Skipper/Owner	Danny Murphy Crosspatrick, Killala
Base	Killala Pier
Telephone	(096) 32249
Length	11.5 m (38 ft)
No. of Anglers	12 maximum
Facilities	Radio, Echo sounder, Radar, Navigator, Toilet, Washup, Cooking Facilities
Daily Charter	£120
Daily Individual	£15
Weekly Charter	By arrangement
Tackle Hire	£5 per day for both Shark and Ground

■ NOTABLE CAPTURES

Species	Weight (lbs)	Location	Bait	Boat/Shore	Date
Grey Gurnard	2.02	Killala Bay	Mackerel	B	7/87
Mackerel	2.58	Killala Bay	Mackerel	B	8/87
Red Gurnard	2.33	Killala Bay	Mackerel	B	8/88
Tub Gurnard	6.31	Killala Bay	Mackerel	B	7/88
John Dory	5.50	Killala Bay	Feathers	B	7/88
Homelyn Ray	5.69	Killala Bay	Mackerel	B	8/90

■ IRISH RECORDS

Species	Weight (lbs)	Location	Bait	Boat/Shore	Date
John Dory	7.5	Killala Bay	Baited feathers	B	8/84
Megrim	4.10	Killala Bay	Baited feathers	B	8/87

COMMON SPECIES

Common Species	Average Size Caught (lbs)
Blue Shark	45
Cod	5
Whiting	1
Gurnard	2
Conger	15
Pollack	6
Ling	8
Tope	25
Ray	9
Dogfish	2

TACKLE SHOPS

John Walkin, Tone Street, Ballina, (096) 22442. Frozen bait available.
V. Doherty, Bridge Street, Ballina
M. Swartz, Ballina Angling Information Centre, (096) 21850

CLUBS AND CONTACTS

Killala Bay SAC: Paddy Gallagher, Rehins, Ballina, Co. Mayo, (096) 21345
General Humbert SAC: Hallie Quinlan, Barrack Street, Killala, Co. Mayo, (096) 32357
Sunset SAC: Leslie McMaster, Main Street, Enniscrone, Co. Sligo, (096) 36103
Moy Estuary SAC: James A. Garvey, Casement Street, Ballina, Co. Mayo, (096) 21138

COMPETITIONS

Killala Bay has been the scene of many major tournaments. The local clubs organise a number of festivals and events annually. Further details from club secretaries.

Sligo & Donegal Bay

S ligo is a county which gets quite a lot of visitors, drawn mainly by the spectacular scenery, fine traditional music and the connections with our greatest poet, W.B. Yeats. Strangely enough, angling tourism is not highly developed and what there is of it concentrates on the fine game angling and the surprisingly good pockets of coarse fishing. Sea angling seems to be a minor interest with both visitors and local people in Sligo Bay, though it has been developed in the part of Donegal Bay which is in north Co. Sligo.

The potential for sea angling with a taste for exploration seems to be there. The patch of rough ground in Sligo Bay called 'The Ledge' is an excellent mark, mainly known for Tope, though I'm sure my old friend Des Brennan will forgive me for remembering the Skate he played for two hours here— until it turned out to be a stone! I have also fished for Flounder in the maze of sandy channels in Ballysadare Bay and wished I had more time to work out the tides and marks and really crack this fascinating bit of water.

And there's no doubt that the enterprising angler who does set out to explore this area will get a great bonus in the freshwater fishing. Lough Gill is well worth the coarse fishermen's attention, but Sligo also has some excellent and little known Sea Trout fishing. The Drumcliff River, either near where it joins the sea or near where it leaves the lake, can be very productive; inexpensive day tickets are freely available.

Donegal Bay is huge and actually has a three-county coastline: a bit of north County Sligo, a tiny bit of Leitrim and, of course, County Donegal. It's a huge bay, open to the west which means it's far from sheltered. In fact some of its beaches develop such impressive breakers when the big Atlantic rollers crash in, that surfers from all over Ireland make pilgrimages to them.

The seaside village of Mullaghmore in north County Sligo is at the head of the bay and is a place I thoroughly recommend. It's pretty, with a good support structure of shops, including a tackle shop, restaurants, and accommodation of all classes and bait. It's off the beaten track, though it can get a little crowded at the height of the summer, and has an excellent tidal harbour with a charter boat operator and a good dinghy-launching slip. As well as access to the whole inner bay from boats, there is a variety of shore angling from beach and rock marks. Above all Mullaghmore has that indefinable character which makes it a place where, the moment you see it, you know you'd like to spend a couple of weeks' holiday there. And, if you bring the family with you and they have limited interest in fishing, there are plenty of other activities in the area.

Bundoran, on the Leitrim-Donegal border, is not a great sea-angling town but is well developed in other ways as a holiday resort and a good base from which to sample the really excellent day-ticket Salmon fishing on the Drowes River or to fish for Trout in Lough Melvin. Having said that, I remember once going for a walk over the rocks just north of Bundoran on a calm day and finding myself staring into the eyes of an enormous Bass which was nosing around in the bladderwrack.

The estuary of the Erne between Ballyshannon and the sea is a lovely wild place where I have had some good Flounder fishing. But its chief claim to fame in my memory is for fly fishing for Sea Trout in salt water. There is something very strange about wading in the sea with Trout fly fishing tackle. Most of the fish I have caught doing this have been Finnock and quite small, though larger fish are taken and a friend of mine has had small Salmon in the surf. The fly pattern is Rogan's Gadget, tied by the famous firm of Rogan's in Ballyshannon town.

There is some good Tope fishing off Donegal town, though, once again, it is a freshwater species that makes this area memorable for me. Lough Eske, just behind the town, has what is, to my knowledge, the only rod and line fishery for Char in the country. These rare cousins of Salmon and Trout have flourished there since they were stranded by the melting ice sheets and are a source of great confusion to the fishery board legislators since they can only be caught in November, when game fishing seasons have all closed.

But Killybegs, the largest commercial fishing port in the country, is really the sea angling capital of Donegal Bay. Its history as a sea angling centre goes back quite a way and it used to have an extraordinary August Festival which was noted for the numbers of politicians who were wined and dined, taken out in a charter boat and brought back looking very green!

It's a busy port and there's certainly never any problem about getting fish bait. In fact it's the main source in the country for fish oil for rubby-dubby. As well as the registered charter operators, there are plenty of boat owners who rent craft on an occasional basis.

The fishing itself offers plenty of Blues and definite recent reports of Porbeagles. The Teelin Knoll is the best-known of the deep water marks for ground fishing, but there are plenty of others and more are being discovered every season. Shore fishing is developing, with excellent Ray marks as well as Flounder, Wrasse and Conger. As you might expect in a busy fishing harbour like this, there is very good Mullet fishing. The Irish record Mullet was taken off Killybegs pier.

All of this, the wild scenery of Donegal, a hinterland full of Sea Trout and Salmon and the quiet hospitality of Donegal people; Killybegs may be a long way away for most anglers, but it's worth the trip.

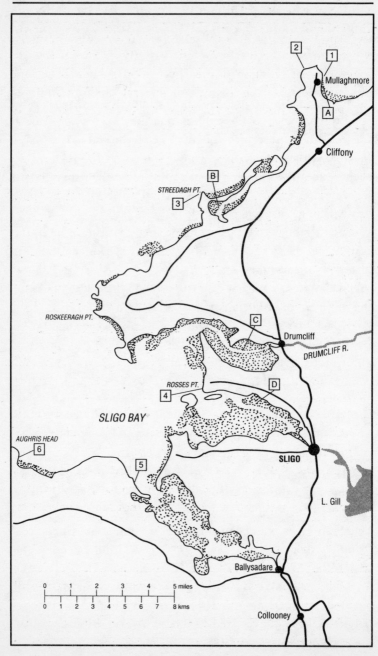

■ DESCRIPTION: AUGHRIS HEAD TO MULLAGHMORE

The coastline in this area is dominated by the large estuaries which drain into Sligo Bay. Until recently, little was known about the sea angling in the area, but with the arrival of several charter boats and the upsurge of interest in shore angling, much has been learned. The area, however, still has much 'undiscovered' fishing available.

■ SHORE ANGLING MARKS (map – page 212)

1. MULLAGHMORE PIER: Mullet to specimen size from pier. From the breakwater: Dab, Flounder, Plaice and occasional Ray in summer.
2. DARBY'S HOLE: Excellent rock fishing for big Wrasse, Pollack, Conger.
3. STREEDAGH: Beach fishing for Flounder, Ray and Dogfish, particularly at night. From the point, a large boulder-stream causeway, there is excellent spinning for Pollack to 8 lbs and float fishing for Wrasse to over 4 lbs.
4. ROSSES POINT TO DEADMANS POINT: Spinning for Mackerel, Sea Trout and occasional Bass. Bottom fishing at slack water for Dogfish, Ray and occasional Tope.
5. PORTROYAL: Sea Trout and Mackerel in summer. Occasional Ray and Tope on evening tides. Flounder very plentiful, as are Mullet in hot weather.
6. AUGHRIS HEAD: Fishing from the beach for Flounder, Ray and Dogfish. Large fish have been hooked on this beach, but not landed. These were thought to have been Tope.

■ BAIT (map – page 212)

A. MULLAGHMORE HARBOUR: Lugworm at eastern side of wall.
B. MILK HAVEN ESTUARY: Lugworm and white ragworm at the top end of the bay.

C. CARNEY: On the channel banks of the Drumcliff River, below the bird sanctuary, lugworm and clam are plentiful.

D. Lugworm are plentiful in the mud along the channel at the Sligo/Rosses Point Road.

◼ APPROVED BOAT FOR HIRE

Boat Name	Aquastar Fisherman
Skipper/Owner	Thomas McCallion, 22 McNeill Drive, Sligo
Base	Raughley or Rosses Point
Telephone	(071) 42391
Length	10 m (33 ft)
No. of Anglers	12 maximum
Facilities	Radio, Sounder, Navigator, Toilet, Washup, Cooking Facilities
Daily Charter	£120
Daily Individual	£15
Weekly Charter	By arrangement
Tackle Hire	Shark outfit–£5 daily; Bottom outfit–£4 daily

◼ NOTABLE CAPTURES

Species	Weight (lbs)	Location	Date
Blue Shark	116 lbs	Mullaghmore	8/89
Blue Shark	119 lbs	Mullaghmore	9/91

◼ COMMON SPECIES

Common Species	Average Size Caught (lbs)
Tope	30
Thornback Ray	8
Pollack	7
Coalfish	3
Blue Shark	70
Conger	11
Ling	6
Dogfish	2

■ TACKLE SHOPS

Barton Smith Ltd, Hyde Street, Sligo
F. Nelson and Sons Ltd, 42 Castle Street, Sligo

■ CLUBS AND CONTACTS

Mullaghmore SAC, Joe Magowan, The Hill, Mullaghmore,
Cliffony, Co. Sligo, (071) 66267
County Sligo SAC, Gerard Devaney, Lisheen, Knocknahur,
Strandhill, Co. Sligo, (071) 68046
Raughley SAC, Bianca Schiller, Ardtarman Castle, Ballinfull
PO, Co. Sligo, (071) 63284

■ COMPETITIONS

Interest in competitive boat angling has been revived in this
area with the formation of County Sligo SAC and Raughley
SAC who between them organise a number of events annually.

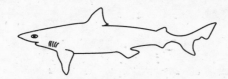

■ DESCRIPTION: KILLYBEGS AND DONEGAL BAY

Killybegs, Ireland's premier commercial fishing port, has also
emerged as one of the top sea angling centres. Both boat and
shore anglers will find a good variety of fish to try for. Several
100 lbs+ Blue Shark are recorded every year while the
springtime Cod fishing is exceptional. Light tackle enthusiasts
will enjoy Pollack fishing over many of the inshore reefs, while
the inner reaches of Donegal Bay, particularly adjacent to
Mountcharles, provide excellent spring Tope fishing. The main
channel which runs all the way up to Donegal town has also
turned up Monkfish recently.

The annual Killybegs festival, one of the oldest on the
calendar, is held every July and attracts a large number of
visitors to the town.

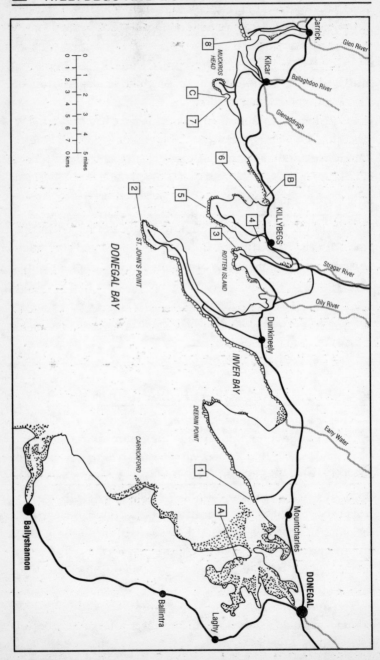

■ SHORE ANGLING MARKS (map – page 216)

1. MOUNTCHARLES PIER: Bottom fishing at high water into main channel (distance casting) for Ray, Bull Huss, Dogfish and occasional Tope.
2. ST JOHN'S POINT: Spinning for Pollack, Mackerel and Coalfish. Bottom fishing for Wrasse and occasional Conger. Specimen Wrasse recorded.
3. GUNWELL: Bottom fishing from rocks over sand for Ray, Dab, Flounder and Conger. Spinning for Mackerel, Pollack, Coalfish. Float fishing for Wrasse.
4. KILLYBEGS: Freelining and float fishing for Mackerel, Pollack and Mullet from east pier. Bottom fishing inside angle of west pier for Conger. Specimen Mullet recorded.
5. DRUMANOO HEAD: Fishing from various rock platforms for Mackerel, Pollack, Wrasse and Conger.
6. FINTRA STRAND: Bottom fishing in channel for Flounder and spinning for occasional Sea Trout. Dogfish, small Codling and occasional Ray at night.
7. TRABAWN: Beach fishing for Dogfish, Plaice, Dab, small Turbot and Flounder.
8. TEELIN PIER: Bottom fishing for Conger, Dab, Flounder and Dogfish. Spinning for Mackerel and Coalfish. High water best. Specimen Conger recorded.

■ BAIT (map – page 216)

A. MURVAGH: Lugworm in estuary behind golf club.
B. FINTRA: Sandeel and lugworm on the banks of the channel.
C. TRABAWN: Sandeel on beach at low tide.

SLIGO & DONEGAL BAY

217

■ APPROVED BOATS FOR HIRE

Boat Name	Niamh Og	Martin Og	Fine Girl
Skipper/Owner	Enda O'Callaghan St Catherines Road, Killybegs	Michael O'Boyle Old Road, Mountcharles, Donegal	Pat O'Callaghan 'Siochan', The Glebe, Killybegs
Base	Blackrock Pier, Killybegs	Mountcharles Quay	Blackrock Pier, Killybegs
Telephone	(073) 31288	(073) 35257	(073) 31569
Fax			(073) 31691
Length	11 m (36 ft)	8 m (26 ft)	11 m (36 ft)
No. of Anglers	Shark–6; Bottom–10	8 max	Shark–8; Bottom–10
Facilities	Radio, Sounder, Toilet	Radio, Sounder, Navigator, Toilet,	Radio, Sounder, Navigator, Toilet, Washup, Cooking Equip.
Daily Charter	£85	£80 (£40 min.)	£85
Daily Individual	£15	£10	£15
Weekly Charter	£480	£500	£340
Tackle Hire	Shark outfit– £5 daily, £20 weekly; Bottom outfit– £3 daily,	Tope and bottom outfits–£5 daily, £35 weekly	Bottom outfit– £2.50 daily, £10 weekly

Boat Name	Bangor Crest	Suzanne
Skipper/Owner	Teelin Harbour Charters Carrick Upper, Carrick	Brian McGilloway Roshine Road, Killybegs
Base	Teelin Pier	Blackrock Pier, Killybegs
Telephone	(073) 39117	(073) 31144
Length	10 m (32 ft)	10.25 m (34 ft)
No. of Anglers	Shark–6; Bottom–10	Shark–6; Bottom–10
Facilities	Radio, Sounder, Radar, Navigator, Washup, Cooking facilities, Toilet	Radio, Sounder, Radar, Washup, Cooking facilities, Toilet
Daily Charter	£85	£85
Daily Individual	£15	£15
Weekly Charter	By arrangement	By arrangement
Tackle Hire	All rods £2 daily. Lures for sale	Shark outfit £5 daily; Bottom outfit £3 daily

Boat Name	Persistence	Arctic Cloud
Skipper/Owner	Enda O'Callaghan St Catherines Road, Killybegs	Anthony Doherty The Glebe, Donegal Town,
Base	Blackrock Pier, Killybegs	Blackrock Pier, Killybegs
Telephone	(073) 31288	(073) 21630
Length	9.1 m (30 ft)	10 m (31 ft)
No. of Anglers	Shark–6; Ground–10	8–10 max
Facilities	Radio, Sounder, Toilet, Washup, Cooking Equipment	Radio, Colour Sounder, Fishfinder, Toilet, Washup, Tea and Coffee provided on board
Daily Charter	£85	£80 (8 persons) minimum charge– £45
Daily Individual	£15	£15
Weekly Charter	£480	£400 (6 days)
Tackle Hire	Shark outfit–£4 daily, £20 weekly; Bottom outfit– £3 daily, £15 weekly	£3.00

NOTABLE CAPTURES

Species	Weight (lbs)	Location	Bait	Boat/Shore	Date
Cuckoo Wrasse	1.26	Killybegs	Mackerel Strip	B	8/87
Red Gurnard	2.25	Donegal Bay	Pirk	B	8/88
Pollack	12.95	Killybegs	Mackerel Strip	B	8/86
Cod	26.50	Killybegs	Feathers	B	5/87
Ballan Wrasse	5.19	Killybegs	Ragworm	B	9/88
Cuckoo Wrasse	1.87	Donegal Bay	Mackerel	B	5/91
Blue Shark	116	Killybegs	Mackerel	B	8/87
Blue Shark	105	Teelin Knoll	Mackerel	B	8/89
Blue Shark	106	Donegal Bay	Mackerel	B	9/90
Flounder	3.19	Teelin Bay	Lugworm	5	9/89

IRISH RECORD

Species	Weight (lbs)	Location	Bait	Boat/Shore	Date
Grey Mullet	7.62	Killybegs Pier	Fishbait	S	6/72

COMMON SPECIES

Common Species	Average Size Caught (lbs)
Cod	7
Whiting	1
Gurnard	1.5
Coalfish	4
Pollack	4
Turbot	3
Conger	12
Ling	5
Dabs	.75
Dogfish	2

TACKLE SHOPS

Charles Doherty, Main Street, Donegal, (073) 21119
Eamon Gallagher, Main Street, Killybegs
McBrearty's Fishing Tackle, Kilcar, Co. Donegal, (073) 38036

CLUBS AND CONTACTS

Killybegs SAC, Mrs A. P. Rouiller, The Evergreens,
Aghayeevoge, Killybegs, Co. Donegal, (073) 31137
Kilcar SAC, John Joe McBrearty, Main Street, Kilcar, Co.
Donegal, (073) 38036
Ballyshannon SAC, Christy Higgins, Chapel Street,
Ballyshannon, Co. Donegal

COMPETITIONS

The Killybegs Festival, which has been running for over thirty
years, is staged in mid July every year. A much more recent
innovation is a Species Competition which is staged in August.
The Kilcar club also organise several events each year out of
Teelin. Details on all local events can be obtained from club
secretaries.

The Rosses &
North-West Donegal

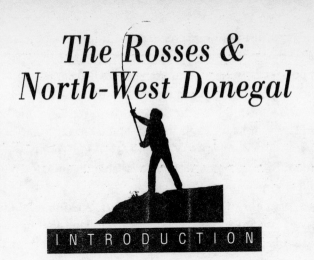

INTRODUCTION

West Donegal, including the coastline of The Rosses, is probably the least utilised stretch of our entire seaboard as far as sea angling is concerned. Its hinterland with its maze of small rivers and lakes and its summer clouds of midges also offers some of the least-known quality Salmon and Sea Trout fishing in Europe.

So this is country for the explorer. Huge potential, few anglers, not a lot of information. If you have a car and you like using Ordnance Survey maps and charts and puzzling out marks for yourself, if you prefer to collect your own bait, if you get satisfaction out of using your own hard-earned knowledge and experience to work out where a species is likely to be at a certain stage of the tide and how it might be caught — west Donegal is the place for you. And if wonderful empty scenery is a bonus, you couldn't find anywhere better.

Shore anglers will find a full range of coastal types from shallow beaches to deep water rock marks. And there is certainly huge boat fishing potential for the angler who tows his own dinghy or can do a deal for a boat with an inshore fisherman. There are some wonderful reefs around Aranmore

Island and in the Owey area. Interestingly enough Bunbeg used to be a sea angling centre years ago, but the sport has died out. Some of the old information about marks should still be there if you find the right people to talk to.

Farther north the angling is a little more developed. The only place in Ireland where anglers still take consistent catches of Haddock in numbers and quality is around Tory Island. But a wide range of other species is available, including Cod into double figures.

It's probably the fact that the north Donegal coast is relatively easy to access from Northern Ireland that has led to the development of several sophisticated charter boat operations in the area. Some of these operators have been concentrating on the potential offered by the large number of wrecks left by the north Atlantic convoys in the two world wars and they've been getting some exciting catches. Irish records will certainly be broken over these wrecks in the next few seasons and if you like wreck fishing or are interested in specimens then this part of the country is well worth a visit.

The 'Garden' east of Sheephaven is a mark which is particularly famous for the variety of species it can offer in a single trip.

A glance at the map shows that north Donegal is deeply indented with sheltered bays, a bit like south Connemara or parts of west Mayo. These bays are attractive to the visiting sea angler because they mean that he will get some sport even if there are Atlantic gales for the whole duration of his visit.

The shore angler is not quite so weather dependent and, though he will be operating with slightly less information than the boat angler, he will find plenty of quality fishing. Some of the Ray marks over sandy sheltered ground are particularly good.

Lough Swilly, with its annual summer angling festival, is probably the top place in the country for pack Tope in large numbers. If you've never caught a Tope and have an ambition to do so, try and get there in July or August. I doubt if you'll be disappointed. And try also to organise a trip out to the wreck of the *Laurentic*, a sister ship of the *Titanic* which was torpedoed and crippled during the First World War and limped in to the mouth of the Lough where she sank. She was carrying gold bullion in her cargo and I'm told every bar of gold has been salvaged by divers — except one! You may not hook the missing gold bar but you're likely to contact some mighty Conger.

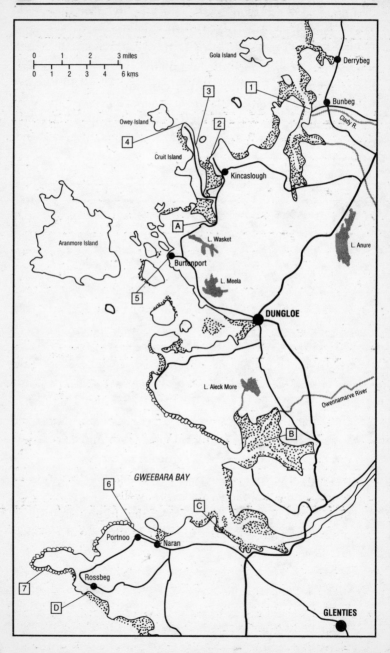

■ DESCRIPTION: WEST DONEGAL AND THE ROSSES

Interest in sea angling (particularly shore fishing) has increased over the last decade. However, much of this area remains under-fished. It is potentially one of the best all-round sea angling areas in the north-west.

Boat angling offers a wide range of species from very diverse locations, including offshore reefs, pinnacle rock, sand banks and shallow estuarine situations.

■ SHORE ANGLING MARKS (map – page 224)

1. BUNBEG HARBOUR: Float fishing from quay wall at high water for Mullet. Pre-baiting brings best results. Spinning from outer wall for Pollack and Mackerel. Bottom fishing for Conger at night.
2. KINCASLOUGH PIER: Spinning for Mackerel, Pollack and Coalfish. Bottom fishing for Flounder, Dab, Conger and Codling. Float fishing for Mullet. Night tides best.
3. CRUIT SOUND: Bottom fishing over sand from rocks opposite Inishillintry Island. First two hours of flood tide and first hour of ebb best for Flounder, Dogfish, Ray and Tope.
4. CRUIT POINT: Spinning from large rock platform over very deep water for Pollack, Coalfish and Mackerel. Bottom fishing for Wrasse, Dogfish and Conger.
   Caution: Cruit Point should only be approached in calm conditions as it is dangerous in sea swells.
5. BURTONPORT QUAY: Bottom fishing from quay wall at night for Conger. Float fishing for Mullet, small Coalfish and Pollack.
6. PORTNOO: Fishing over sand from rock platform west of pier for Dogfish, Plaice, Dab, Flounder, Ray and small Turbot. Spinning for Mackerel, large Sandeel and Pollack. Float fishing for Wrasse. Two hours either side of high water best.

7. DAWROS HEAD: Bottom fishing over very rough ground for Dogfish. Spinning for Pollack, Mackerel, Coalfish and occasional Garfish.

■ BAIT (map – page 224)

A. KEADEW STRAND: Lugworm and clam on channel banks.
B. TRAWENAGH BAY: Lugworm, white (herring-bone) ragworm on banks of channel.
C. WHITE STRAND: Lugworm. Sandeel in vicinity of O'Boyles Island.
D. ROSSBEG: Lugworm and herringbone ragworm on bank of main channel. Crab around base of rocks at mouth of bay.

■ BOAT FOR HIRE

No charter boats are available at present, but several commercial fishermen can be booked on a part-time basis (mainly at weekends) at Bunbeg, Burtonport and Kincaslough.

■ NOTABLE CAPTURES

Species	Weight (lbs)	Location	Bait	Boat/Shore	Date
Torsk	6.44	Burtonport	Mackerel	B	5/90
Torsk	9.47	Burtonport	Mackerel	B	5/90

■ IRISH RECORD

Species	Weight (lbs)	Location	Bait	Boat/Shore	Date
Torsk	10.35 lbs	Burtonport	Mackerel	B	5/89

COMMON SPECIES

Common Species	Average Size Caught (lbs)
Cod	7
Tope	25
Whiting	1.5
Gurnard	2
Haddock	2.5
Coalfish	6
Pollack	5
Turbot	7
Bull Huss	8
Lesser Spotted Dogfish	2

TACKLE SHOPS

Charles Bonner, The Bridge, Dungloe, (075) 21163
John Magill, Main Street, Ardara

CLUBS AND CONTACTS

Gweedore SAC, Dan Friel, Magheraclogher, Bunbeg,
Co. Donegal, (075) 31333
Rossbeg SAC, Martin Tonry, Kilclooney, Portnoo, Co. Donegal

COMPETITIONS

Gweedore SAC generally runs a number of events throughout
the season. Further details from club secretary.

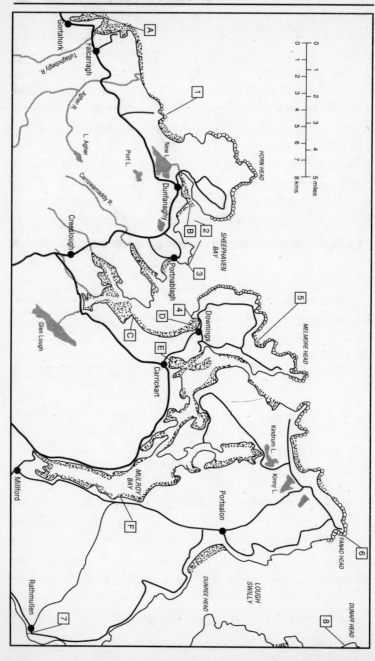

■ DESCRIPTION: NORTH-WEST DONEGAL

This area offers some of the best shore angling in Donegal and Ray fishing in particular can be outstanding at marks on Sheephaven Bay and the Inishowen Peninsula.

Boat anglers have a wide range and variety to fish for, including excellent offshore angling for Cod and Haddock and shallow water fishing for species such as Tope, particularly on Lough Swilly. Inshore dinghy fishing is a popular pastime, with holiday makers angling at Portnablagh, Downings and Rathmullen. Wreck fishing is emerging as a real tourist attraction, particularly out of Rathmullen and Culdaff.

■ SHORE ANGLING MARKS (map – page 228)

1. DOROS POINT: Spinning from rocks on flooding tide for Mackerel (in season), Pollack, Coalfish and occasional Sea Trout. Bottom fishing from rock onto sand or from beach for Dab, Flounder, Codling and occasional Bass. Distance casting produces Dogfish and occasional Ray in summer.

2. DUNFANAGHY: Spinning in main channel for Sea Trout and bottom fishing at low water for Flounder. Surf fishing on main beach for Dab, Flounder, Coalfish and occasional Codling and Bass, particularly in autumn.

3. PORTNABLAGH: Rock fishing to the north of the harbour for Wrasse, Coalfish, Pollack and occasional Conger. Distance casting onto sand for Ray, Dogfish and Flatfish.

4. DOWNINGS PIER: Bottom fishing at high water for Dogfish, Flounder, Dab and occasional Plaice. Fishing close to the pier for Conger, especially at night. Float fishing for Mullet, small Coalfish and Pouting. Spinning for Mackerel in summer.

5. TRA-NA-ROSSAN: Bottom fishing into deep water over sand from rock platform on south-west side of bay for Ray, Dab, Dogfish, Gurnard. Spinning for Pollack, Mackerel and occasional Sea Trout. Steep climb down from road. Surf

fishing on beach for Coalfish, Flounder, Dogfish and occasional Ray. Rock fishing over very foul ground on northern side for Conger, Pollack, Wrasse and Mackerel.

6. FANAD HEAD: Spinning from finger of rock on northern shore over very foul ground for Pollack, Coalfish and Mackerel. From the rocks to the south of the lighthouse, spinning accounts for Pollack, Mackerel and Sea Trout. Fishing close to the rock produces Wrasse and Coalfish, while distance casting over sand turns up Dab, Dogfish and Codling.

7. RATHMULLEN PIER: Spinning for Mackerel in summer. Bottom fishing close to the pier for Conger and over sand for Flounder and Dogfish. Occasional Tope and Ray can be taken while distance casting. Night tides are most productive.

8. DUNAFF HEAD: Rock fishing for Pollack, Wrasse, Conger and Mackerel.

■ BAIT (map – page 228)

A. BALLYNESS BAY: Lugworm on banks of river channel. Razor fish can be dug at the extremity of spring tide strips. The area around Ards Point is most productive.

B. DUNFANAGHY: Lugworm and small white ragworm south of channel.

C. CREEVAGH: Lugworm on banks of channel; crab around base of rocks.

D. TRABEG: Lugworm, very deep in sand. Single digging necessary. Some white ragworm, sand eel and razor fish on spring tide strips.

E. CARRICKART: Lugworm in estuary to south of Island Roy. Clam also present.

F. CARROWKEEL: Lugworm on mudflats north of caravan park. Clam also present.

■ APPROVED BOATS FOR HIRE

Boat Name	Charlie Girl	Pegasus II	Barracuda
Owner	John McLean Cullion, Letterkenny, Co. Donegal	Malcolm Bowden Meenreagh, Rathmullen, Letterkenny, Donegal	Inishowen Boating Co Ltd, Carrowmore, Malin
Base	Portnablagh Harbour	Rathmullen Pier	Bunagee, Culdaff
Telephone	(074) 22443	(074) 58282 (074) 22585	(077) 70605 Fax (077) 70764
Length	9.1 m (30 ft)	10 m (33 ft)	10 m (33 ft)
No. of Anglers	Shark–5; Bottom–7	Shark–6; Bottom–10; Wreck–6	Shark–8 Bottom, Wreck–12
Facilities	Radio, Sounder, Navigator, Toilet, Washup, Cooking Equip.	Radio, Sounder, Radar, Navigator, Toilet, Washup, Cooking Equip.	Radio, Sounder, Radar, Navigator, Toilet, Washup, Cooking Equip.
Daily Charter	£90	£100 (£70 min. charge)	£150
Daily Individual	£15	£10	£15
Weekly Charter	£500	£280–400 weekly by arrangement	By arrangement
Tackle Hire	Shark–£4 daily, £25 weekly Bottom–£3 daily, £18 weekly	Bottom outfit– £2.50 daily, £10 weekly	£3 daily

■ NOTABLE CAPTURES

Species	Weight (lbs)	Location	Bait	Boat/Shore	Date
Red Gurnard	2.30	Downings	Mackerel	B	8/89
Red Gurnard	2.06	Rathmullen	Mackerel	B	7/90
Blue Shark	144	Downings	Mackerel	B	8/90
Blue Shark	124	Downings	Mackerel	B	8/90
Red Gurnard	2.26	Culdaff	Mackerel	B	7/89
Megrim	2.13	Tory Island	Lug and Herring	B	7/87
Monkfish	55	Lough Swilly	Mackerel	B	6/91
Pollack	12.85	Rathmullen	Eel	B	8/91
Ballan Wrasse	5.47	Moville	Ragworm	B	8/91

COMMON SPECIES

Common Species	Average Size Caught (lbs)
Cod	7
Whiting	1.5
Gurnard	2
Haddock	4
Tope	25
Coalfish	6
Pollack	5
Turbot	7
Bull Huss	8
Spurdog	5
Lesser Spotted Dogfish	2

TACKLE SHOPS

The Post Office, Rathmullen
D. McLoughlin, 7 West End, Buncrana
B. O'Neill, Bridgend, Lifford Post Office
Eamon Martin, The Border Shop, Lifford

CLUBS AND CONTACTS

Donegal County SAC, Joseph Stubbs, 3 Ballyraine Park,
Letterkenny, Donegal, (074) 22055
Downings Bay SAC, Trevor Ryder, Gortamore, Downings,
Co. Donegal, (074) 55261
Fahan SAC, Wm Grant, West End Bar, Buncrana, Co. Donegal,
(077) 61747
Fanad Orchard SAC, John Logue, Rossnakill, Letterkenny,
Co. Donegal
Foyle SAC, Gerry Sona, Drumowen, Moville, Co. Donegal
(077) 82278
Glengad Malin SAC, Tony McDermott, Carrowreagh Road
Carndonagh PO, Co. Donegal, (077) 74345

Lough Swilly SAC, Niall Doherty, 'Beverly Hills', Ballybol, Rathmullen, Co. Donegal, (074) 58129

■ COMPETITIONS

Several popular tournaments are staged throughout the year at Portnablagh, Downings, Culdaff and Rathmullen. These are mainly boat competitions, but shore angling events are growing in popularity. Details from club secretaries.

Central Fisheries Board
Balnagowan
Mobhi Boreen
Glasnevin
Dublin 9
Tel: (01) 379206

South Western Regional Fisheries Board
1 Nevilles Terrace
Masseytown
Macroom
Co. Cork
Tel: (026) 41222

Eastern Regional Fisheries Board
Mobhi Boreen
Glasnevin
Dublin 9
Tel: (01) 379209

North Western Regional Fisheries Board
Abbey Street
Ballina
Co. Mayo
Tel: (096) 22623

Bord Failte
Baggot Street Bridge
Dublin 2
Tel: (01) 765871

South-Eastern Regional Tourism Organisation
41 The Quay
Waterford
Tel: (051) 75823

Shannon Free Airport Development Co. Ltd
Shannon Town Centre
Shannon
Co. Clare
Tel: (061) 361555

Shannon Regional Fisheries Board
Thomond Weir
Limerick
Tel: (061) 55171

Southern Regional Fisheries Board
Anglesea Street
Clonmel
Co. Tipperary
Tel: (052) 23624

Northern Regional Fisheries Board
Station Road
Ballyshannon
Co. Donegal
Tel: (072) 51435

Western Regional Fisheries Board
Weir Lodge
Earl's Island
Galway
Tel: (091) 63118

Dublin & Eastern Regional Tourism Organisation
1 Clarinda Park North
Dun Laoghaire
Co. Dublin
Tel: (01) 808571

**Cork/Kerry Regional Tourism
Organisation**
Tourist House
Grand Parade
Cork
Tel: (021) 273251

**Western Regional Tourism
Organisation**
Aras Failte
Galway
Tel: (091) 63081

**Donegal-Leitrim-Sligo Regional
Tourism Organisation**
Aras Reddan
Temple Street
Sligo
Tel: (071) 61201

**The Irish Specimen Fish
Committee**
Balnagowan
Mobhi Boreen
Glasnevin
Dublin 9
Tel: (01) 379206

**Midland Regional Tourism
Organisation**
Dublin Road
Mullingar
Co. Westmeath
Tel: (044) 48761

**Paul Harris
Irish Tourist Board**
Angling Representative
47 The Crescent
Brinklow
Nr. Rugby
Warwickshire, CU23 OLG
England
Tel: (0788) 833203

INDEX OF MAIN PLACES